# The Errand Runner

Design: Brant Cowie/Artplus

CANADIAN CATALOGUING IN PUBLICATION DATA

Rosenberg, Leah.
  The errand runner

ISBN 0-471-99874-5

1. Rosenberg, Leah. 2. Jews in Canada—
Biography. I. Title.

FC106.J5R67      971'.004924     C81-094382-4
F1035.J5R67

Printed and bound in Canada
10 9 8 7 6 5 4 3 2 1

# The Errand Runner

*Reflections of a Rabbi's Daughter*

**LEAH ROSENBERG**

 **John Wiley & Sons Canada Limited**

Toronto   New York   Chichester   Brisbane

# Dedication

This book is dedicated to the memory of my parents, Rabbi Jehudah Yudel Rosenberg and Sarah Gitel Rosenberg, and the future of my grandchildren and great-grandchild.

Heartfelt thanks and gratitude to my editor Sarah Swartz who guided me and edited the manuscript with skill, devotion, patience and love.

Many thanks to my grandniece Sandra Schwartz Maker for her sustained support and encouragement.

Thanks to Mel Hurtig for his interest and assistance.

To my brother Rabbi Abraham I. Rosenberg for his advice and help.

And sincere gratefulness to my publisher who made a dream come true.

# Contents

## *Prologue*

WHEN MOSES LED THE JEWS out of Egypt, they wandered forty years in the desert before they could reach the Promised Land. The truth is that this goal could have been attained in a matter of days. But the Jews had to learn understanding, to master the power and reasoning of Talmudic Law that would enable them to conduct themselves within that Law. And they had to shed years of slavery and bondage.

In a way I too was a slave, albeit a willing one, to my Judaism. I was tied to a rabbinical and Chassidic background from which there was no escape. I devoured it; it was as much a part of me as living and thinking. It nourished me; it gave me substance, vibrance and joy. Though my roots went very deep, ultimately I was compelled to accept the fact that there existed a world other than that of my immigrant parents. I did not want these two worlds to be in conflict; I yearned to reconcile and combine the two. How would I accomplish that feat? Integrate? But how was it possible to integrate without betraying my heritage? How could I accept the new without relinquishing the old?

Ringing in my ears was mother's constant admonition, "Leah, do not ask questions. It is a sin." Then father, "Leah, one must seek and ask questions." Whose advise should I follow? I began to reason that my own intellect had to be my guide. It was I alone who could decide the direction of my life. I would do things *my* way and be responsible for my actions and for my mistakes. I could no more stop thinking than stop breathing.

As the years went by, I began to understand that integration need not mean giving up one's identity. We barter and exchange our heritage with others. To me, integration is a way of forming vibrant and lasting links in a new land. We must accept each other without prejudice. Each must learn from the other of beliefs that will enable us to participate and understand and communicate.

As a result, I not only did not give up my heritage, but I learned to share it. I wear my Jewishness like a badge of honour. I talk incessantly about festivals and customs and *kashrut*, till my neighbours now have Jewish calendars so that they know the Jewish festivals and proudly inform me when they occur.

Like the Jews in the desert, I could have shortened the journey. But it took time for me to learn, to accept, to respect, to understand, to forego bigotry. It was painful, but I grew. Now I want to travel back in my life. By going backward, I may come forward.

To protect the reticent members of my family, I have given them all new names. But they are all here. I could not tell my story without them.

PART ONE

# CHAPTER 1

## In the
## Old Country

NOTHING IN THE WORLD is so pulsating as the memory of the years. Those memories bear witness that I have lived a life. I can relive and be strengthened; I have fulfilled myself. I have brought children into the world. Whether they agree or not, I live in them. I will go on forever in my children and theirs. One day a descendant shall say, "Just look at her! Remember our great-grandmother Leah? Our daughter looks and acts just like her." Away up there in the sky, I shall smile to myself.

Every nerve is electrified by some episode that occurred years ago; I can still feel it. Where shall I begin? There are so many characters in my mind who clamour to be painted and given voice. Lavish is the panorama of my memories.

I was born in Warsaw, Poland, at the beginning of this century, the offspring of generations of rabbis. As the youngest daughter, I was rarely noticed and was thus better able to observe my older siblings. We carry from birth physical and psychic ingredients inherited from our parents. My father often commented that all that was lacking in me to be a fullfledged rabbi was a beard, and, truly, this I have never been able to achieve.

I entered this world on the festival of Shemini Atzares which culminates the Jewish new year observances. It was the wrong time to make an appearance. On the day of my birth, the midwife was busy assisting two other women in labour, and my father was occupied with prayers. The midwife, who had attended my mother before, knew my mother had laboured long in the past. She was, therefore, not in a hurry to come. When she was called to mother, her answer was a refrain: *"Fer de Rebbetzin, es brent nisht."* (For the rabbi's wife, there is no rush.) But I was a fast one, in a real hurry and have not slowed down yet.

It was my brother Isaac who ran to fetch father, and it was father who delivered me. My father never tired of describing the birth to me. His face a study in awe and delight, he would begin, "You see, Leah, you were stillborn and obstinate and refused to cry. I turned you over and gave you a few resounding slaps which made you recognize my authority. You began to scream." At that point, father imitated my cries. "And so," father said, "you are truly my very own daughter."

I came late in life to my parents; I was the youngest daughter. There was some question about my name. Father insisted on Biblical names and decided on Leah. Mother was not too pleased. "Need I remind you," she argued, "Jacob did not want to marry Leah; he loved Rachel. I do not want a similar fate for this child." Father then replied, "Our Patriarch Jacob did very well by Leah; she bore him many sons." I gave birth to two sons, and they made up in quality what I lacked in quantity. And so I became Leah.

My father gave a mystical explanation of birth. In heaven the soul of the infant is taught all the five books of Moses, the Torah. Before its descent to earth, an angel gently taps the infant, and its memory is erased. So you see how it was with me — I resided in heaven prior to being born and, had I been endowed with any sense, I would never have departed.

My maternal grandparents resided in Tarlow, Poland. My grandfather travelled to smaller districts that boasted forests to purchase timber for his employer. Father lived in Skarshov, Poland, a small town from where he brought his sick wife to the larger city, Tarlow, for medical treatment.

It was the custom in those days for Jews who lived in outlying areas to come into larger towns on festivals and during times of adversity. Accommodations were hard to find. Though there were small hotels, money to pay for such luxuries was not easily available and obtaining kosher food was even more difficult. Jews clung together both in misfortune, which was rampant, and security, which was rare. My grandfather who was known for his generosity opened his home and allowed my father, a fellow Jew in need, to stay with his ailing wife. The doctor said they had arrived too late. My father's first wife died soon thereafter, leaving four small children.

My father stayed on for six weeks after his wife's funeral. It soon became obvious to my grandparents that his prolonged visit was directly related to the presence of their daughter — my mother.

It may appear callous that a man should consider remarriage so soon after the death of the mother of his four children. But it must be understood that orthodox Jews believe that a pious and learned man may not remain unmarried. It behooved a young rabbi like my father to wed quickly, lest he harbour unchaste thoughts. It was also thought that a married rabbi could better minister to his congregation. And there were the four motherless children in need of care.

During the entire time my father stayed in my grandfather's house, no direct conversation passed between my parents. The discussions were carried on in separate sequences. My grandfather spoke to my father, then to my mother.

My mother, at that time seventeen, initially was not free to marry. She was already betrothed to a young man who worked as a labourer, and the wedding date had been set. A betrothal was considered almost as binding as marriage. My grandmother, a very practical woman, thought it was a good idea for my mother to wed a man who could support her, a rarity in those days.

Grandfather opposed the match. The young groom had relatives in America, and this was a stigma. Jews who left the impoverished *shtetl* (village) life with its traditions and family ties did so only for unmentionable reasons. It would be years before America could be viewed as a haven and not as a place of exile. Another drawback was the young man's position as a labourer. My grandfather adhered to the rabbinical tenet that an educated man must endeavour to wed the daughter of a learned man and have his own daughter marry a man versed in the Torah. One day in the heat of argument, my grandfather cried out, "Heads will fly, and this *shidech* (match) will not be." Soon after that day, the young bridegroom drowned.

Later, when my father asked to marry my mother, my grandfather called upon his daughter to decide her own fate. This was a most permissive gesture on his part: daughters were rarely consulted about their marriages. My grandfather sternly pointed out, however, "Bear in mind this man is poor and the lot of a rabbi is a precarious one. He is a widower with four children. All you have in him is a Talmudist."

"That," my mother said, "is what I want." Meanwhile, all she was allowed to do was steal glances at my father.

The wedding took place, and great and joyous was their union. The year was 1888.

Marriages in those days were usually not made in heaven. A marriage was conducted with all the pomp and intrigue that is associated today with the merger of complex business concerns.

One profession born of the Jewish way of marriage was that of *shadchen* or *shadchante* (matchmaker). The fine art of matchmaking was respected and even feared in the community. Fate rested in the hands of the *shadchen* who could make or break a *shidech*. These people knew well how to capitalize on their position. The *shadchens* would often appear at a home on the Sabbath with the pretext of proposing a match. Their arrival would coincide with the most sumptuous meal of the week for the most impoverished families would deprive themselves all week to enhance the Sabbath. The parents of marriageable children would greet the matchmakers with, *"Gut shabbes*, Rab Nussen, just in time to grace our Sabbath meal," or "Yente, how lucky are we that you happened to be near our house for the Sabbath." It was a ritual practised with finesse and craft. Discussing money matters on the Sabbath was not allowed, and so the happy matchmakers would relish their feast without talk of dowries or settlements.

The bride's parents were expected to provide a dowry. A dowry could be settled as *nadan*, an actual sum of money, or as *kest*, residence and support of the young couple in the home of the bride's parents. The majority of dowries, however, took the simplest form of *tzigezoogt* which translates best as promises and were usually executed with wonderful "intentions".

Marriage was entered into at a very early age. The groom was seldom older than eighteen and could not be expected to earn a living. Dowries were most important for this reason. The worth of a young man depended heavily on his aptitude for learning and status as a scholar. The most coveted groom was the *yeshiva bucher* (Talmudic scholar), next was the *melamed* (teacher), followed by the *mohel* (circumciser), *shoychet* (ritual slaughterer), and *baal tfileh* (conductor of prayer services).

A *nagid* (man of wealth) would take great pains to marry his daughter into a family of *yiches*, those of rabbinical or scholarly background and the equivalent of aristocracy in the community. We were the people of the book, and knowledge was afforded the greatest honour. The *nagid* was regarded with respect, not for his material acquisitions, but for his potential accomplishments in the way of *tzedaka* (charity).

A family who could not marry into *yiches* for some reason would settle for a groom who was an *am ha-aretz* (man of the earth) and worked with his hands. As a wage earner the *am ha-aretz* had a broader selection of brides, not having to be dependent upon a dowry. Among the Jews it behooved the community to protect and care for orphans and widows. When a poor girl was to marry, the rabbi would often approach a *nagid* to provide a dowry.

When the *kest* was over, the young couple would leave the home of the bride's parents, sometimes before the husband was capable of earning a living. It was common for the wife to become the breadwinner. There was never a stigma attached to such an arrangement. A wife who could provide for her family was held in great esteem, for, through her efforts, her husband was able to pursue his study of the Talmud.

Enough cannot be said of Jewish women in their triple roles of wife, mother and provider. The women devoted their lives to their families without complaint, and like the prophets of old, they held aloft the banner of Judaism, the Torah. The survival of our culture and religion rested on the shoulders of these women who cooked, cleaned, bore children and worked in the market place to provide their menfolk the opportunity to study the Torah and pass on the strength of the Jewish people from generation to generation.

It is worthy of note that the Jewish wife as a breadwinner was not cast in a role that was forced on her. Nor did she accept it as her lot in life. Rather, she understood and recognized it as an implication that she was a helpmate to her husband.

There were factors she could have resented. Foremost among those was the idea that she had to produce a son. The true fact was that the male child was received with greater joy than the female one. Yet that had no bearing on the love for the child. Once a son was born, the sex of the next child held little significance.

The Jewish wife possessed an implicit comprehension of herself as a woman. As her husband was shaped by Talmudic studies, she relied on her *Tseno-Ureno*. This was a book of several volumes written in the purest old Yiddish, paraphrased from the Pentateuch and read aloud every Sabbath, as my mother read it to me. It was almost magical in its effect. It was a book of knowledge, a fountain of wisdom, a guide to moral behaviour. It brought to life the Patriarchs, the wisdom of King Solomon. It taught how to raise children and keep the home in a traditional manner.

While totally aware of herself as a woman, the Jewish wife never questioned her security. That irksome prayer recited each morning by men—"to thank God that I was not created a woman"—passed her by. She was aware that men played the major role, but to her this was a form of protection. While she did not define the word sex, she kept her sexual relationship with her husband sacred. She memorized the phrase repeated by her father: "And the bridegroom shall find pleasure in his bride."

The Jewish wife as a mother fulfilled herself. Without reserve she gave and gave. Like my mother, she either nursed or carried during most of her young life. The boys were enrolled in *cheder* (Hebrew school) at a tender age. The girls were taught to run the home with *yiddishkeit* (Jewish tradition)—to greet the Sabbath, to light the Sabbath candles, to observe the rules of modesty and sanctity, to keep a kosher home and above all to obey. And somehow it all worked.

Before my parents married, my father sent his four children to live with his sister. He always spoke with love of that sister. It became a joke with my parents when they disagreed, father would sigh resignedly and say, "What a pity my sister Perele is no longer with us. She would soon tell you that I am always right."

A few months after the wedding when mother was already pregnant, she approached father concerning his children. She wanted them brought home. "When I married you, I knew there were four children and you cannot leave them indefinitely with your sister. If we have them when they are still young, they will regard me as their mother." Sadly, they never called her mother. In many Jewish homes it was the custom to address the stepmother as "aunt". Though my mother was willing to accept my father's children, somehow they were never able to regard her as their mother.

I believe that there are two kinds of resentment; one, the product of love, the other, the product of hate. The latter almost needs a manufactured motive. It lies dormant in the former, then swells and hardens. This was the case with mother's stepchildren. The older ones had to contend with prettier daughters and more promising sons. What dark thoughts did they harbour through the years? Superstition told them that my mother's thoughts had induced the death of father's first wife at the time of her severe illness. Perhaps they believed that their own mother died because mine yearned for a learned husband.

Many years later at my father's funeral I walked hand in hand with Hannah, my father's oldest daughter from his first marriage. To my extreme horror she said, "Everything has to be forgiven, even father's second marriage. If he had not brought his sick wife to your grand-father's house, my mother would have survived." I was so shocked that I could not trust my ears. I had no reply. Surely, one was not expected...it no longer mattered. This bitterness must have been lodged in their hearts over many years.

My father moved his family from Tarlow, to Lodz, and finally to Warsaw. His fame spread and he soon became known as an *eileh* (genius). Those years were a terrible struggle. My mother gave birth fourteen times but only seven children survived.

My mother often recalled the tragic death of my little brother, Yankele. He was killed at the age of ten, felled by a stone. No one knew whether it was an accident or not. Jews lived in a pall of fear. A police investigation was unheard of. My mother spoke of Yankele's death, and always a great sorrow flowed from her.

My youngest brother, Israel, was a surviving twin. I vividly recall the time when the other twin died at the age of ten months. My father sat up all night next to the table where the small body lay. His wavering voice broke with grief but he continued reciting the psalms, huddled over his dead child all through the night. It was as if he thought the child would be afraid to enter the other world. He wanted his son to know that the voice and presence of his father accompanied him wherever he was bound.

Life was very difficult to sustain in Poland. The pogroms were a constant danger, and poverty, especially among the Jews, was becom-ing unbearable. In 1912 my father left for Canada to establish a home for us. He reasoned that life in Canada would be much easier. The struggle for mere existence would be over, and the family would not have to live under the pall of fear that hung over European Jewry. Mother and we children stayed in Warsaw to await his summons. I was sent to an aunt and uncle who were affluent and childless.

My aunt was a stunning woman with startling red hair and flashing green eyes. She wore the long gowns of that era and the large brimmed hats with feathers and carried a walking stick. One time she dressed to go to a wedding. I remember she wore a long pastel gown, and a sheet was placed on the floor so that her hem would not be soiled. I can still see her standing before a long mirror turning this way and that to admire the effect.

My uncle was the capitalist of the family. He and his wife resided on a main thoroughfare on a street called Nalevki which goes by the same name today. Their sumptuous flat contained both their living and business quarters. The merchandise consisted of delicate lace by the yard. The proximity of home and business enabled me to watch daily the monetary proceedings. My aunt and uncle allowed me the freedom of the house.

It was during my stay in Warsaw that I remember becoming conscious and self-reflective. I didn't share my thoughts with anyone and little attention was spared me in the midst of business interactions. I was about seven years old and spent my time reading and contemplating the world around me. I remember looking out a window wondering how, while the window was small, I could see objects much, much larger.

Everything fascinated me. I marvelled at my vision. I thought: I have two eyes which can see so much. I looked in all directions so that I would miss nothing. I was in awe of the people around me. I compared one person with another and watched their behaviour. I thought and I thought, but I did not ask questions. I felt everyone was so occupied they would not give answers. The usual conversation with my aunt and uncle consisted of, "Leah, why are you so quiet?" Or my uncle would say aside to my aunt, "She never says a word." Everything I looked at, I associated with people.

It was customary for wealthy people to have *oyrechim* (guests) at table on the Sabbath and on festivals, usually *yeshiva buchers* and poor men. It was incumbent upon Jews to have places prepared at their tables in readiness to welcome those who needed their hospitality. Even poor families did their best to adhere to this custom. My relatives were very generous and always had an abundance of *oyrechim*; and the festivals were made merry indeed by their generous hospitality. The table was set with silver cutlery dedicated to the Sabbath and festivals. The silver candlesticks were lit by my aunt. The table was a long affair in the living room which was used as a dining room as well.

My aunt had a sister, Yachebed who also lived with my aunt and uncle. Yachebed in no way resembled my aunt. She was short, round, with a moon face full of freckles. On Fridays before the Sabbath, Yachebed went shopping and took me along. We went directly to a pastry shop. The pastries were mostly made with ground almonds. The cakes were potent with liquor. All the wares were displayed on glass platters.

Before we left Warsaw mother went to make her farewells with relatives. She had an aunt whose husband was to leave after us and make his home in Toronto. His family was to follow later. Mother took me with her. It was a painful experience that lodged in some recess of my mind.

In the room where we sat were two curtained windows. I noticed heavy drapes in the centre of the room, and I wondered if those covered another window. Suddenly the drapes parted, and the figure of a young girl appeared. She stood there silent as if she were set in a frame. She was slender and quite tall. Her brown hair was piled up in the fashion of the day. Her dress was brown with high puffed shoulders. It was as if she were about to go to a party. Her face was delicate and heart shaped. Her eyes met mine and clung to me. They were calm, sensitive and melancholy. I was deeply touched and overwhelmed with a sadness that I did not understand.

Later I asked mother about the girl. Mother said, "Leah, she is not with everything." For mother that so-called explanation embraced many situations. "Not with everything" could mean a headache, a contagious disease, a miscarriage or a simple disaster. In this case it was a nervous breakdown. This beautiful creature had the misfortune to fall in love with a young man who was considered an undesirable match.

The aunt never did come to Toronto. She was unable to bring the daughter to Canada with her and could not bear to leave her behind.

# CHAPTER 2

*The Members
of My
Family*

I HAVE AN EVERLASTING LOVE for both my parents. It is many years since they passed away, yet their dear faces hover ever before me. I was blessed with outstanding parents — such people, it seems, no longer exist. They had great spirit, an overpowering urge to survive, to fight for their children, to shelter them and pass on to them a wonderful heritage. I feel that my father gave to each of his children some vibrant ingredient, a vitality that carried on from my generation to the next. I have always felt that I was only a temporary keeper of this spark of life; it was on loan to me to be passed on to my children. In each of my children is imbedded something of the greatness of my father.

My father, my wonderful father, a lion of a man, a king of Israel — he was endowed with all of God's graces. His eyes seemed to reflect on all the misfortunes of the world, and yet they were often full of laughter. His hair was red, his forehead was high and his white skin smooth as silk. His long nose and beard, not too thick, and fragile cheekbones framed a beautifully formed mouth. He was tall, commanding and walked straight until the day he died. His voice was well modulated, and his hands were wonderfully expressive. He raised his voice only when he was aroused by some injustice. I remember him seated in his study surrounded by his *sphorim* (books) and the legions of Talmudic lore. In his hand was a quill pen he had made. When he walked, it was as if he were carried on air, his feet barely touching the ground. He had a potent humour, penetrating and satirical, not bitter, but kind like a benediction. And oh, his smile! It was born in his eyes and meandered from there until it lit up his lovely face like a sun through rain clouds. He was so lovable! His image lives in the fibres of my being and in my heart forever.

Father was the descendant of an illustrious line of Chassidic rabbis, that of a great Cabalist and authority of Jewish law. His ancestry went back to a renowned rabbi who was one of the editors of the *Mishnah* (part of the Talmud, the body of Jewish religious and civil law). Father often spoke of his youth in Poland. His early thirst for knowledge never abated and embraced astronomy, science and politics.

In those years the study of alternate customs was frowned upon by orthodox Jews. My grandparents had an attic in their home. My father, who had studied the Russian language, saved his meagre pennies to buy candles by which light he would read the forbidden Russian books in the attic. Books of a nature not related to the study of the Torah, particularly in Russian, were forbidden by Jewish parents. Russian and any foreign language were associated with pogroms. Even books in Yiddish were regarded with suspicion depending on their contents.

Father practised in the rabbinate and studied homeopathy, the herbal treatment of disease. He also possessed a diploma from a Russian university. He was a *sopher*, a Hebrew scribe who could write religious and official documents such as the scrolls of the Torah, the *Ketubah* (marriage contract), the *get* (bill of divorce), the *Megillah* (Book of Esther), and the *mezuzah* (the prayer "Hear O Israel" which is fastened to the doorposts of Jewish homes). Father was also a *mohel*, a *shoychet* and a *baal tfileh*. To hear him conduct services was to feel the presence of God.

Father translated the *Zohar* (most influential Cabalist text) from Aramaic to Hebrew and wrote many books of Yiddish folklore such as *The Golem of Prague* and *The Story of Spoler Naida*. He also wrote studies of old healing remedies, bewitchery and sorcery. His book *Healing of the Body and the Mind*, concerning the dependency and harmony of the two, is still pertinent today.

My mother was a compact and sensual woman, what we call *zaftig* (juicy) today. She had skin that did not ever wrinkle, even in her bitter and sick old age, and beautiful dark eyes. I never knew the colour of her hair. It was all cut off on her wedding day and was never allowed to grow back as was the orthodox custom. Instead she wore a *shaytl* (wig). Mother was graceful and always kept herself looking beautiful for father. He was her king, the centre of her universe and life revolved around him, his needs and his wants. Mother was the perfect wife for my father. She was practical and down to earth. Though not an intellectual like father, she was very clever, politically minded and knew what transpired in the world.

Mother also traced her ancestry to great Talmudists and Chassidic rabbis. My grandmother was a direct descendant of a Chassidic rabbi who was the disciple and pupil of the founder of Chassidism, Rabbi Israel Baal Shem Tov. My mother was taught the *siddur* (prayer book) in Hebrew and was also fluent and literate in Yiddish. For a woman of her time, she was well educated. She maintained an enormous correspondence with her family in Europe, all of it in Yiddish. Mother believed in *mitzvas* (good deeds) and performed these avidly. I have no idea how she managed with the little money she had to support her great number of relatives. I suppose it worked out somewhat like the manna from heaven which the Jews ate in the desert.

My mother was a compassionate and deeply religious woman. Every Saturday she read aloud from the *Tseno-Ureno* and the portion of the week while I sat beside her and listened intently. On festivals it was always I who accompanied her to the synagogue. While the cantor recited prayers not necessary for us to follow, mother read the special prayers for women to me. Over and over she wept at the same words as though each rendition were the first. Her feelings were greatly distressed by the words, "Do not forsake me in my old age." I was so moved that I cried with her and always remembered her fears.

I see myself sitting beside my mother at synagogue services or listening to her reading the Biblical accounts of Abraham, Isaac and Jacob. The years never dimmed the excitement and pathos of her melodious voice as she recounted the tales of Sarah, Rebecca, Rachel and Leah. Oh, I loved her dearly. Mother was extremely devout, believing that all of life was God's will. She accepted all that fate brought. "If so," I would argue with her, "why should we struggle or exert ourselves?"

The love I bore my mother was not purely a filial devotion. It went beyond and above that. It was not a duty. To me, duty is a cold word, even an ugly one. Yet to mother, duty was a road one had to travel willingly. To struggle was pointless. "That," she often said, "is God's way, and we must obey." I could not make peace with her convictions. Nor could she do the same with mine. She argued with me as I fought back. I yearned to make it clear to her that to think my way did not go against either her or my religious convictions. That is what she feared most.

All the business transactions of my family were handled by my mother, and how she schemed and planned! Hannah, my father's oldest daughter, had to be wed, but there was no money. Mother had exactly five rubles in her bank account but had promised five hundred to the groom. Since this amount was not remotely possible, mother used magic. She added two zeros to her account book, and the wedding took place. Mother agreed that it was an extreme measure, but marriageable daughters called for drastic action. She assured me that hers was not an unusual method. One married off a girl in the name of mercy. The less attractive or capable the girl, the more ingenious the methods of wedding her.

In some cases a groom would arrive with his parents to view the bride. Frequently, it would be the younger and prettier sister preferred for examination. During the wedding ceremony, the bride was traditionally veiled. Imagine the groom's surprise when he discovered, too late, that he had been tricked. Mother assured me that these particular kinds of deception could only occur if the groom lived in a different town—naturally! Shades of Jacob and Leah.

Mother spoke often of the hard life in the old country with a lingering nostalgia. The life in the *shtetl* had a kind of togetherness, the sharing of troubles and good fortune. When reminiscing about those times, mother invariably told the story of Chia Ruchel, a tale repeated each time with the same sighs and incantations, while I interrupted at appropriate intervals with exclamations of disbelief, urging my mother on.

Chia Ruchel was an orphan. Although everyone knew everyone else, no one was quite certain how she reached that state. She just happened. As no one knew her origins, it was naturally concluded that she was a *ness* (miracle). At the age of five the girl simply appeared at the synagogue door. She was adopted by several families on a time plan. As time does not stand still for even a Jewish orphan, Chia Ruchel grew into a beautiful maiden of marriageable age. Among her many suitors was Gershon, son of Reb Reuben, the butcher. Reb Reuben insisted on a *nadan* or he would not consent to the match. The rabbi went to a *nagid* who saw his duty clearly and furnished the dowry.

At this point there would be a pause in the story, while I waited. "Such a wedding," mother sighed. The festivities and feast were seen to by the women of the most affluent families. Then came the description of the wedding itself. The bride sat on the most comfortable chair in the centre of the room. She fasted all day to be in the proper mood for the *badchen* (a gifted man best described as a sort of court jester). He chanted with sadness and humour the joys and pitfalls of marriage. The bride heard about the obstacles, rewards, blessings and sorrows which might await her. This was sung and, most remarkable, it was all in rhyme. The bride wept, the women cried and a glorious time was had.

The *chuppa* (marriage ceremony) over, and the guests seated, a master of ceremonies would stand on a chair and announce the *drusha geshunk* (wedding presents). These contributions were the essentials of life. An *iberbet* was such a gift. This feather blanket was a lifesaver in a cold country that knew no central heating. One could survive without cards, cocktails and televisions in those days, but not without a goose down *iberbet*. *Lechter* (Sabbath candlesticks) were among the absolute essentials bestowed on the newlyweds. How could one usher in the Sabbath without them? The *lechter* often found their way to the pawnbroker during the week, only to be redeemed in the nick of time for the Sabbath lighting.

My parents founded quite a dynasty. From my father's first marriage were Hannah, Selma, Daniel and Sander. My mother's seven children who followed were Baruch, Isaac, Chia, Elie, Riva, myself and Israel.

Both my sisters from father's first wife were married in Poland. Hannah married Shimen, and he was a terror. He never ceased bringing up the matter of the dowry. Hannah would run from him each time seeking refuge with my parents, and it seemed each time with a new baby. Shimen came after her and always took her back.

Shimen was the first of our family to leave for Canada. He found a rabbinical position in Toronto for my father, and thus became the spearhead of our family's odyssey to the "golden land".

Selma, the second daughter, married soon after Hannah. Yossel, her husband, was a watchmaker and a shrewd man of trade. I still remember the wedding. Selma carried a bouquet of red roses and, to this day, when I gather roses from my garden, their scent conjures memories of that wedding day. My sister Selma was the mildest, sweetest of the girls. I don't know from whom she inherited that peaceful disposition. One seldom gave a thought to her looks; she was someone to love.

Daniel was my father's oldest son. Father wanted all his sons to be scholars, but Daniel preferred to learn a trade. When Daniel and his family immigrated to Canada, father, who could do almost everything, taught him to be a ritual slaughterer. This profession required Daniel to study Jewish law. He applied himself to the laws governing *schechita* (slaughter), and he acquired a taste for study which really pleased father.

Sander was the youngest of the first four children. He was the image of my father: tall, slender, graceful and he had charm, personality and a sonorous voice that served him well in making speeches. He was extremely intelligent, well educated and had a biting tongue.

Sander made a rich and glorious match; his wife Chana and her family worshipped him. He received a dowry and *kest* with no limitation of either traditional requisite. He seemed to have a lifelong charge account with payments in advance. The years Sander passed with Chana's parents in Poland were not wasted. He applied himself diligently to the study of the Talmud, received *smicha* (a rabbinical diploma) and was later confirmed by father. When World War I intervened, his family was brought over to Montreal by father.

Outwardly, Sander seemed extremely successful in his chosen field. He went from one rabbinate to another, each time to a more illustrious position in a larger city. But Sander never became part of any community. Though he fulfilled his duties as rabbi and knew the Law, he seemed to lack the human touch.

His biggest problem was in communicating with other rabbis who served neighbouring communities. He had a way of belittling other rabbis to which they did not take kindly. And so after years, the exodus from one city to another was becoming problematic. This upset father whose many years in Canada embraced only two cities, Toronto and Montreal.

Finally, on one of Sander's visits home, father broached the subject with him. "Sander, what is it? Why the constant change of positions and, most of all, why is there so much tension and ill feeling between you and other rabbis?" The reply was startling: "Father, the other rabbis lack common sense; they try to discredit me. Now they have formed a committee which offered me five thousand dollars to leave the city." Quietly father asked, "What was your reply?"

"Well, father, I told them I would pay them five thousand dollars to remain in the city so that their communities could better evaluate their mental capacity and weigh the conclusions against my own intelligence." Father dropped the subject.

My mother's children spanned quite a range of years from Baruch, the eldest, to Israel, my younger brother. My mother's oldest son was Baruch, my parents' love child. I have letters from him written to my parents in Russian and Yiddish. They are so full of love and devotion. Those tender messages seem to live and breathe even today. He sent my parents all kinds of advice about diet and health. He wanted them to live long so that he would be able to love them for an eternity.

Parting with Baruch was very difficult for my parents. My mother recalled that, as our departure to Canada drew near, Baruch came often to the house. When father was about to leave, Baruch removed his shirt before embracing father, so that more of him would be exposed to be covered with kisses and tears. There was a great deal of love between them. No other child played so important a part in the emotional lives of my parents. Their separation from him coloured their daily existence in the years that followed.

Baruch resembled my mother in appearance and my father in mental capacity. He was a university student in Kharkov, Russia. Many Jewish parents tried desperately to place their sons in universities. This meant a tremendous sacrifice, for besides the discrimination that the children faced in acquiring access, they could not as students observe the Sabbath or the high holidays. Orthodox Jews never considered these concessions as even vaguely possible for their children. When the son of a rabbi became a university student, he placed his father's livelihood and reputation in jeopardy.

Baruch was well aware of this. When he came to visit, he wore the uniform of a student, but he would enter the house from the rear so as not to attract attention. He had no desire to threaten the standing of my father in the community, and he knew full well what it meant to be the son of a rabbi.

Baruch suffered from this, but he could not forego his craving for higher, worldly education. He planned to study agricultural engineering and emigrate to Palestine. Baruch became involved with a fellow student, Anna. She also came from a very orthodox family and was the divorced mother of two children. Needless to say, it was much more difficult for women to be students, and Anna was a mathematician, a profession guarded by male students.

Though it was a painful compromise, our parents had to accept Baruch's decision to have a career outside of the rabbinate. Baruch had his plea, "I have a right to live my own life. I will not enter the rabbinate." Baruch's resolve was bolstered by the fact that he was admitted to the university. Hundreds of Jews applied for entrance; a mere few made it.

Sander had a real hatred for Baruch. His loathing for Baruch resembled that of Joseph's brethren. The thought that his father loved Baruch more became an obsession with Sander. He could not abide it. Though he had everything going for him, Sander felt that Baruch had usurped his place in father's heart, a place for which we all vied.

I recall a scene which my parents did not know I had witnessed. My father, unaware that mother was listening, heard Sander's usual poisonous remarks about Baruch. On this particular occasion, Sander was holding forth on the dangers to which a rabbi was subject by having a son at a university. He insinuated that father was leaving for Canada because he could not possibly earn a living with such a disgrace hovering over him. "No community," Sander said, "would tolerate such a rabbi." I cannot remember what my father answered but my mother stepped in and a violent argument took place. Sander's face was flushed with defeat, for what victory can one brother hope to gain over another?

I always think of my brother Sander with anguish. I loved him dearly. There were characteristics about him that I found wanting, but who am I to judge? Perhaps in assessing character there is no right and no wrong. It could well be that Sander was sincere in his feeling that Baruch posed a threat to father. Also, from his religious perspective, he regarded Baruch as a deserter of Judaism. Perhaps his reactions then were not only motivated on the basis of the brother to brother relationship.

Isaac was my mother's second son. He was very like my father. He wasn't very tall, yet it seemed that a slice of father had been reproduced in Isaac. From earliest boyhood, he would disappear without warning. He joined the various revolutionary movements which flourished at that time. Always he returned destitute, bedraggled and hungry. Isaac was a constant source of despair and worry to my parents. On one of his appearances, he brought a gun back from his foray. Father tried to reassure us that it contained no bullets, but to my parents, there was nothing more terrifying than this instrument of violence.

Somehow Isaac and my parents managed to survive this period. In later years, whenever Isaac came to town, he would rush home to see my father. He would greet him with such emotion that mother and I would leave the room. His feelings and tears would drain us.

Isaac was the most lovable of my brothers. He had great depth and many gifts. He was able to give of himself and to love us all — how we adored him! He was a wonderful mimic and would portray Isaac blessing Jacob, or a prophet admonishing the people. He could have us in stitches playing a *mitnagid* (opponent of Chassidism) quarreling with a Chassid.

Born in approximately 1895, he was just past twenty when he arrived in Canada in the spring of 1914 with his bride, Vera. A tiny, thin girl with a mass of auburn wavy hair and a face full of freckles and emotion, that was Vera.

Theirs was a good marriage. They were ideally matched. Vera was already a fine actress and later matured into a poetess, an art she still practises in her eighties. She had a beautiful voice. One was astonished at its impact. When I first heard her sing, I looked to see where the powerful voice came from. I could not imagine such vibrance from so tiny a frame. That voice earned fame and considerable fortune. Isaac and Vera worked together all through their lives. He wrote the plays, and Vera starred in many of them.

As soon as father was convinced that Isaac was not for the rabbinate, he tried to wean him from the theatre. He sent him to a tailor shop to learn that trade. Isaac worked one week and earned three dollars which he promptly framed.

Father could not imagine how Isaac could earn a livelihood from writing and theatre. Nevertheless, Isaac lived his life the way he wanted. He was fortunate to see all his brain characters come to life. His mind was forever at work. While our father produced Talmudic works, Isaac wrote plays in a similar beautiful script, each letter a pearl.

Father and Isaac were at odds in their thinking, yet a strong bond existed between them. All through Isaac's life, he gathered material pertaining to father. It was Isaac who made it part of his work to bring father's books of folklore within reach of the masses.

We were four sisters from father's second marriage — Chia, Elie, Riva and myself. Chia, the eldest, was our mother's daughter. There was a strong bond between them. It endured through their lifetime. Chia remained faithful to her orthodox upbringing. She never faltered. We were friends, and in many ways Chia guided me through much of my life. She had a great feeling for all of us.

In character Chia was soft and pliable. While bereft of English schooling, she had an inborn intelligence that enabled her to follow her children's education for which she strived and fought. Her knowledge was acquired from the Yiddish newspapers which she read religiously. There was an aura about her, a luminous quality that drew people. I loved her.

Chia felt a precise attitude towards her destiny as a woman and her duties as a daughter, wife and mother. She excelled in all of them. "Marriage," Chia said, "that is the ultimate goal. Respect is what you must give to your husband." The emphasis on respect was a contention between us that was never resolved. "Respect must be earned," I argued.

I had in my young years more contact with my sisters Elie and Riva. We were closest in age and attended the same school. But there was a great deal of friction between these sisters and myself. They revolted against orthodoxy which they regarded as an encumbrance. What they felt hampered them was being immigrant girls. But it was their ridicule of Judaism which I found most difficult. They had every right to their thinking, I kept repeating to myself. Yet it was a thinking that I could not understand, and I constantly criticized them for the anxiety they caused our parents.

Another area of disagreement between myself and my two sisters was the difference in our attitudes towards school. Elie and Riva longed to leave as quickly as possible, while I was of a completely different opinion.

I remember an incident related to school which occurred when I was eleven, Riva was fifteen and Elie was seventeen. Due to a minor illness, I was absent from school. I required a note to excuse my being away. They wrote my note, and I, in my innocence, never bothered to read it.

My teacher was a Miss Petrie; both my sisters had been in her class. Miss Petrie was an unmarried lady in her early fifties. She was a dignified, elegant lady who would not tolerate any nonsense. She was tall and angular and seldom smiled. To win her recognition or a favourable remark on one's work was like being handed a medal. We all stood in awe of Miss Petrie; we revered her.

I handed Miss Petrie the note and stood at her desk. As she read it, her colour rose. She turned to me, "Leah, who wrote that note?"

"My sisters," I replied. She made no further remarks. When I got home Elie and Riva confronted me with deep mirth. I learned that the note contained reference to her spinsterhood in a deprecating, insulting manner.

I always thought Elie the most attractive of my sisters and the most gifted. She was an introvert and held herself aloof from all of us. It took years for Elie and myself to form a strong friendship. Always she sat deep in thought, while I suppressed a desire to ask what she was thinking. Elie was a real beauty; there was nothing usual about her. Her face was oval; she had black hair, almost black eyes, and a lovely white skin with a beautiful mouth. She watched her figure years before people thought of diets. She had a tremendous feeling for style.

Where Elie had a tranquillity about her, Riva was the complete opposite. There was an electricity about her, a restlessness. She was exciting and determined to get the most out of life. This did not detract from her. Riva had enormous sex appeal, and she used it. She resembled mother closely in looks, but not in character. Plumpish, lovely complexion, roundish face with eyes that roamed back and forth, as if to weigh the possibilities of a situation, she was and still is beautiful. In later life, she was an excellent business woman, sold her stocks before they dropped and bought before they rose.

Unlike as my two youngest sisters were, there was a great similarity between them. They were alike in their attitudes. They were alike in their roles as mothers. Strong as a rock was their battle to give their children every opportunity to succeed in life.

A ferocity assails me when I remember the potentialities of the girls — Chia, Elie, Riva. I long to turn back the years so they could have a second chance. As I look back on our lives I am still beset by the pain I always felt that Elie and Riva, who were so capable, were not able to attain the positions in life that their qualities entitled them to. But it was a time when daughters were trained only to be wives and mothers, and my parents did not rise above those aspirations for us.

Israel, my youngest brother, was born seven years after me. He and I received the best of father's attention possibly because the older children had left home and my father was then more relaxed in his position within the community.

Israel was sent to a rabbinical *yeshiva* (Jewish school for higher learning) in New York. Each time Israel returned home, father assessed his progress. Eventually, this process terminated with father taking over the task of preparing him for the rabbinate.

Israel was a scholar, a product of our father's teaching. Father could be likened to a prosecuting attorney. He questioned and steered Israel through *The Guide to the Perplexed* by Maimonides, *Shulchan Uruch* (Code of Jewish Law) and *Tosafot* (additional critical and explanatory notes on the margin of the Talmud). In addition, from father's constant presence, Israel derived an understanding of humanity, a spirituality.

Israel thrived on this diet. Every remark my brother uttered was translated into an allegory that personified rabbinical studies. Around it, was an air of urgency. Israel had to apply and receive *smicha*. It was a holy, happy, fulfilled event of celebration for my dear parents.

Today Israel is an exponent of our father's way of life. He is surrounded by father's library and mementos. He and mother are in every corner of his study. He lovingly follows the teachings of our father, reveres his memory and treasures the *kapote* (long black satin coat) and *shtreimel* (round hat trimmed with fur) which our father left to him. He humbly wears them when chanting father's favourite prayers.

To me, it is a miracle that Israel was successful in his career. He had much to contend with from early childhood. He was considerably handicapped by mother's love and ambition for him — a love that was transcended by mother's love for father. She had to justify herself in father's estimation by giving him a son who was a rabbi. Ever present in her mind were the images of the two pious sons of father's first wife and the reality of her Baruch and Isaac who had strayed from the fold. Mother's hopes centred around Israel.

I believe what worked in Israel's favour was his complete unawareness of the pressure situation in which he was innocently involved. Added to that was his aptitude and desire for learning and his love for both our parents.

Israel is possessed by father's image. It is hard to say whether that has hampered or fostered his career. It is an influence his fine mind has never in the slightest detail cast off. In that respect my brother and I are more alike than ever. We often talk of our parents. Nothing in our lives can substitute for the love, devotion and memory of them.

There sits my brother surrounded by historical Judaica antiques and impressive paintings of Jews in prayer shawls and phylacteries. Father's picture is right behind him and dominates the room. I regard Israel seated in his study with a volume of Talmud open with a bookmark, and I see father. There is a strong resemblance; he has mother's colouring, and brown eyes that are deep but lack father's penetrating glance. He has inherited father's humour and beautiful script and a measure of father's warmth that enables him to involve himself in the problems of the community.

I ask, "Israel, did you know why mother pushed so hard for you to become a rabbi and if you did, do you harbour any resentment for her actions?" He gives me a deep look, "I did not become aware of that till father passed away and mother agitated for me to remain in Montreal to take father's place. I sensed that it was only her love for me; she wanted to make certain I had a rabbinical position. I loved her dearly, and I am deeply grateful to her." Then he broke into a laugh, "I wonder if I succeeded due to her supreme devotion or my own efforts."

The children of a father who has achieved greatness automatically vie for his love. We hungered for my father's praise and for his attention. I don't think he ever realized how much we were in competition with one another. There was a distinct aura of rivalry between the two sets of children. Though my mother tried to treat the older offspring with equality, they must have resented the love my father showed my mother.

Mother's problems were rooted in her feelings about father. She worshipped him. When neither Baruch nor Isaac had followed the rabbinical tradition, she felt that she had failed father. It became almost an obsession with her that she give father a son who would follow in his footsteps. Actually, it went even deeper than that, for she was in competition with my father's first wife. It was a silent battle — a controversy which never took physical shape but never abated for one moment.

Father was completely unaware of the conflict that raged in mother's heart and mind. It was as if a dead woman wielded an ominous power over her life. It also had an alarming affect on her health. The mother of Daniel and Sander had fulfilled her role; my mother's only desire was to achieve as much.

PART TWO

# CHAPTER 3

## Immigrant Life
## in Toronto

THE JOURNEY TO CANADA made a deep impression on me. My mother and her five youngest children — we four girls and Israel — travelled via Holland on the ship *New Amsterdam*. Fortunately, we left Warsaw in 1913, the year before the beginning of World War I. Mother was terribly seasick, lying on her bunk, barely managing to keep track of her brood. She feared we would arrive in Canada motherless. At least we knew father would be meeting us in Toronto.

Most of our fellow travellers were bound for the United States, and only a small percentage for Canada. To the question: "Where does a Jew travel?" the unanimous reply was: "America, the golden land." But the names of new cities and towns still meant less than the streets back home. Most of us were young, as the time for bringing over older relations was in the future. Oh, we dreamed of the *shifs karten* (passage fare) that would reunite children and parents and bring back the flavour of the old country. Imagine the nostalgia that was carried on the ship for country, childhood and youth.

I was remarkably healthy on the crossing. I walked about holding on to ropes and well remember their rough hemp texture. I ate heartily at the long reserved tables of kosher food and was able to indulge in my favourite pastime — training my eyes and ears on people. I listened as they voiced their fears and watched as they drew together for warmth and reassurance. Lifelong friendships developed and people referred to fellow passengers as *shif shvester* and *bruder* (ship sister and brother).

In the cabin next to ours were three young women in their early twenties. They were *kallehs* (brides) bound for men they hardly knew or had never seen. The three were forever talking and whispering during the night. Shifra was older than the other two and more sure of herself. She was destined for the brother of her brother-in-law, and this gave her a sense of security and position of authority. Masha, too, was going to marry a relative, a second cousin living in New York whom she had met when he had visited her *shtetl* to approve the choice.

Brina was the quiet one. She had light brown hair and delicate features, and her eyes — seldom did a smile lurk in them — gave her an elusive, worried quality. Brina knew absolutely nothing about the man whom she was to marry. All she had was an address of a small town in the state of New York. She had been selected by the head of the *yeshiva* where her future husband had studied, and she knew only that he had the profession of *mohel*.

I would often see Brina reading and found myself constantly trailing her about. She would ask, "Leah, why do you look at me so solemnly?" I was drawn to her, and I felt there was an affinity between us. In fact, there was a similarity in the design of our lives. I met Brina years later. Her husband came to my father for help because Brina had become withdrawn and unreachable. Their marriage had been an unhappy one and they had only one little girl — a melancholy child much like her mother.

So we passed our time on board the ship. We glanced surreptitiously at the upper decks and were rewarded with a glimpse of the first- and second-class passengers. I guess we were awed by what we considered a life which we could never hope to attain.

We arrived at long last and landed on Ellis Island in New York where our troubles began. Immigrants were obliged to have a small amount of money with them when they arrived. My father who was already in Toronto was aware of this and had entrusted the money to Shimen, Hannah's husband, to send to my mother in Poland. Shimen never sent this money, and so we were detained.

The shipping company provided food for one day only. There we were — mother and her brood of children with no food, no money and no place to stay. Mother was upset, afraid and enraged. Through an interpreter, mother managed to telephone father. She had vowed never to speak to him again in her anger. The money finally did come through, a great deal more than was necessary. Before we got on the train for Toronto, mother bought an abundance of food: salami, bread and bright red apples. All through the journey, she kept up a litany of *"Ess, kinderlech, ess"* (eat, children, eat).

We left Warsaw on October 18, 1913, and arrived in Toronto on October 30. The autumn colours still adorned the trees. There was a peace and beauty that we felt immediately in our new homeland. Father had rented a large house on busy Agnes Street by the corner of University Avenue, and this became our new neighbourhood.

In the ensuing years our home was our sanctuary. There were ten rooms, and we were ten people. That did not give each a room for there was father's study, the waiting room which served as a synagogue during festivals, the dining room which was the family room and the kitchen. The bedrooms were all shared, as were the beds.

In addition to my parents, the four girls and Israel, there was an uncle who had accompanied father to Canada who lived with us. The year after our arrival, my brother Isaac joined us with his wife Vera. They lived with us for several years.

Life was very difficult for immigrants. We were called *greener* (new-comers). People worked hard, and not one family occupied a house alone. Everyone took in boarders, usually single men who awaited their families. These men shared the family life in the homes where they stayed, while they worked hard with the driving determination to send for their wives and children. The woman of the house would add the extra food these boarders required to her shopping excursions. Then she would put more meat in the pot and more water in the soup. In spite of the difficulties, there was generosity, commonalty, shared sorrow and joy. Everyone aided each other. The style of life between families and boarders became the fabric and the foundation of the new life in a free country.

Our home became a stopover for relatives far removed who were on their way to every corner of Canada and the United States. Our walls seemed to stretch to receive more newcomers. Not only were all our beds occupied, but we children often slept on mattresses on the floor.

My mother had an incurable thirst for relatives. One day a woman in her sixties.came to consult father. My mother was struck by the fact that this woman's appearance, short and round, was so similar to her own. Mother dramatically declared this was the stature of all her relations. Ultimately this woman's son married my sister Elie.

The bulk of father's earnings came from marriages, divorces and circumcisions. Salaries, if they existed, paid rabbis mere stipends. We had no washing machines, only washboards, and who had heard of a vacuum cleaner? Who could even afford carpets? It was only urgent that one lit the Sabbath candles and baked *challah* (braided bread). Despite the abundance of chores, everything came to a halt on Friday afternoons. The Sabbath was ushered in, and the synagogues filled.

In those years immigrant families were observant Jews, and orthodoxy was the pattern. The Sabbath and the festivals played an important part in people's lives. There was the preservation of the kosher laws, shops closed Friday afternoons and Jewish women went to the *mikva* (ritual bath). Traditions and roots were deeply implanted.

The heart of Jewish life still reposed in the synagogues. I recall how awed I was by the large Orthodox synagogue on University Avenue. Within our immigrant community, Conservative ones were not as yet visible, and Reform was not in the Jewish vocabulary. Small *shtibls* (synagogues over stores) flourished and became gathering places. There were "societies", each comprised of *landsleit*, people from the same towns in Europe.

Queen's Park was where the young congregated. Here the youth and even the middle-aged mingled, argued and planned for a better world. Jews felt a deep love for Canada, a reverence. Queen's Park was their haven, their meeting place to extoll their "Kanada" and voice their hopes. Living was hard, but not without possibilities.

The Jewish community in Toronto was divided into factions. These divisions, and the hostility between them are hard to comprehend today. Jews came from very small towns in Europe, and it is understandable that they clung together. Each group also chose a rabbi from their own town or district.

There existed a deep division between Jews from Poland and Jews from Russia. Polish Jews had lived in isolated *shtetls* and ghettos. Even their pronunciation of Yiddish was different. The speech of the *Polishe* had a lilt and singsong that made them the butt of the Russian Jews.

Polish Jews were mostly of Chassidic adherence. Such a Jew, given a choice between a lucrative business deal or an afternoon visit to hear his *rebbe* "talk Torah", did not hesitate. The choice would be his *rebbe*. Generally Russian Jews were *mitnagdim* (opponents to Chassidic Judaism), and though Chassidim regarded *mitnagdim* with tolerance, even with sorrow, the latter held Chassidim in contempt.

Chassidism is a religious mystical movement that arose in Eastern Europe in the eighteenth century. It was proclaimed and promoted by a man of menial trade, a lime digger, Israel ben Eliezer, who was a gentle mystic known as the Baal Shem Tov. His philosophy was that life is a joy and that happiness was not dependent on knowledge or wealth, but only on communication with God. Man was created in God's image and was a part of God. This rendered each one the right to approach God and confer with Him.

Its success was attributed to the fact that it arose at a time when the Judaism was passing through an era of stagnation in the ghettos. Chassidism was almost a revolutionary movement; its emergence produced a rejuvenation, a rebirth. It provided Jews with the strength to face life and endure the perpetual persecutions that persisted in Europe.

My father was a Chassidic rabbi. Through him, I learned to love Chassidism passionately. Father inculcated me with the wisdoms of the *Zohar* and *Cabala*. I was, and am, held in its warm embrace, protected by its armour against the ills and conflicts of life. Chassidism is to me a form of rapture directed towards God. It is a way of regarding life as a miracle in all its diversity. We are born to experience life with its strife, sorrow, poverty, bereavement, beauty and blessedness. For this privilege we render thanks to our creator. We Chassidim share our joys and our sorrows. We are closely bound.

There is a profound difference between a rabbi and a Chassidic *rebbe*. While the former was ordained by diploma, the *rebbe* had to arrive at his exalted position by descent. While the rabbi had to be conversant with "Law", the *rebbe* devoted himself to the study of *Cabala* (mysticism).

The *rebbe* is a petitioner of God on behalf of his people. He officiates for the rich, poor, old and ailing. Often a person suffering from mental illness would claim that his body was possessed by a *dybbuk* (evil spirit). The *rebbe* was then called upon to perform the exorcism. The Chassidic followers of the *rebbe* would not transact a business deal, buy a home or sanction a marriage without first consulting their *rebbe*. He is the business adviser, psychiatrist, matchmaker and, on occasion, physician of his followers. The *rebbe* seeks to communicate with God on behalf of his people. This requires devout and soul-searching meditation. He must be clever, pious and understanding.

Most *rebbes* were known by the name of the town from whence they came. Many are the disputes between Chassidim as to the greatness and powers of their respective *rebbes*. There is an old story of two men who met at a wedding. They each began to extol the virtues and miracles performed by their chosen *rebbe*. In the heat of the ensuing argument, they almost came to blows. Each man claimed that his was the greater *rebbe*. Finally a third man drew them apart, and when he asked the two to name their leader, it was discovered that they were both followers of the same *rebbe*.

My father was both a Chassidic *rebbe* and an ordained rabbi. He wore the long black satin coat called a *kapote*. Around his waist he wore a *gartel*, a black belt made of silk twine, to separate, symbolically, the upper and lower body. He always wore white socks and a wide brimmed black hat. On Sabbath and festivals, he wore a round fur hat called a *shtreimel*.

Father became known as the *"Polisher rebbe"* and, in the sect-torn community of Toronto, he ministered to the Jews from Poland. On Saturday afternoons our home was filled. A barrel of beer on tap in the yard awaited guests. As I watched, the men went out to fill pitchers with beer. It was an unusual environment for a young girl. No wonder I am a peculiar woman.

The rabbis assembled in our home on Saturday nights after the *habdala* (benedictions said at the conclusion of the Sabbath). It was the time for talk of politics, current events, community affairs and even some of the more petty jealousies of the rabbinical community — after all, rabbis were human too!

Those nights I loved! Mother prepared hot tea with lemon slices in tall glasses. I served the tea, but I was never able to figure out how they tolerated lifting those hot glasses. I would seat myself quietly in a corner and listen. I observed the faces of those who gathered in our home as they spoke and emphasized some passage in the Talmud. Their hands would fly back and forth with fingers dancing as they made their point. Their pure delight in discourse was wondrous to behold. Through the years I have witnessed people at many so-called "joyous gatherings", but I have yet to find such genuine pleasure, such nourishing of the soul or such love for learning!

The climactic moment of the day arrived when the *shalosh seudot* was served. This is a meal eaten before the Sabbath ends. It consists of various delicacies, such as *gefilte fish*, *arbes* (chickpeas) and *kichel* (small cookies). It was father's custom to leave *sheriim* (leftovers). The men seated around the table vied with one another to possess the smallest morsel of food father had touched, for it was believed that he had cast a special benediction on such food. Father would be asked to interpret intricate passages in the *Mishnah* (code of civil and religious law) or the *Sedrah* (portion of weekly reading from the Pentateuch). He would clarify how the Law was instrumental in leading us to an understanding of our lives that we might better learn to cope. The men listened enthralled for hours.

Then, the miracle! As long as I live, this scene will not be erased from my memory. Father slowly rose, and as he did, so did all the other men. At this time they began to sing, all the while covering one ear with a hand. They stood and, simultaneously each one placed a hand on the shoulder of the man next to him. Slowly, slowly, they left the table, formed a circle and started to dance. In a special rhythm each moved in harmony with the others. Their faces lit up with an indescribable aura of rapture and sublime joy. They looked fulfilled, as though freed from all earthly anxieties. It was a mystical sight to behold!

Artists often came to visit my father. They made sketches of him, painted him and interviewed him. Foremost were the writers like Sholem Ash and Peretz Hirshbein. I can only vaguely recall the latter, but I can see Sholem Ash before me right now. He came every year, usually on Purim or Simchat Torah. He favoured the happy festivals. He was always accompanied by a secretary who sat and took notes, as if he were afraid that any word uttered would be lost or forgotten forever. Ash was a warm man and, although the "notes" made appearances in his books, he did not visit for ulterior motives alone.

I remember one of his visits particularly well. He arrived late at night, and we were in bed asleep. Mother came upstairs and woke us. She told us that Sholem Ash was in the house and wanted to see how much we had grown since his last visit. Downstairs we marched. He lined us up against a wall indicating our height at last "inspection". He remembered all our names, and we loved him. He was such a very gentle man.

The most gratifying and unforgettable days of my girlhood were the celebrations of the festivals. I loved Passover most of all. So many overwhelming incidents still cross my mind. My memories of those happy days of my youth are so much a part of my heart and my mind that I could not continue to live without them, any more than I could survive without vital organs.

The festival of Purim occurs four weeks before Passover. It is recorded in the Book of Esther how Haman plotted to annihilate the

Jews. They were saved because Esther had married King Ahashverus, and her uncle exposed the villainous Haman before it was too late. So we rejoice. One of the joys of Purim is the tradition of *shlachmunus* (gifts). On our table seed cakes and honey cake, wine and cognac are set. The *schlachmunus* are mysterious, usually brought to our home by a child. Gifts are covered with napkins and carried on glass plates so that one does not know what delight is contained thereon. There were often gifts of money, and mother came to rely on these for the coming Passover festivities.

Best of all were the many performers who came to grace our table. Young girls came dressed as Queen Esther, accompanied by young boys who played her uncle Mordecai and Haman. They showed deference for father, and when he smiled, they were so pleased that their faces glowed. They sang and danced and performed their little plays while father sat and watched. Purim as it was meant to be! I have never experienced a Purim since as it was celebrated in my parents' home, and I never will. When my parents grew older and festivals were relegated to memories, we would recall those years as a general recollects his victories.

Succot was the feast of the gathering of the harvest. Orthodox Jews ate in the *succah*. This was a booth decorated with citrons and apples constructed outside, under the sky. The roof was of heavy green foliage. The male members of the family ate their meals in the *succah*. Even in chilly weather father would sit shivering in the booth, his collar turned up, his face wreathed in smiles. Our *succah* stood intact in our yard from year to year. Like the Jewish faith, it lived through storms — not even a snowstorm could destroy it.

Mother would describe a *succah* in the old country. This communal *succah* was erected from year to year. Wives carried the meals into the *succah*. Mother related with a note of sadness that many deprivations were experienced to make those meals presentable. It meant precious objects found their way to the pawnshop before the festival. Appearances had to be kept up, and the festival had to be celebrated according to God and to man.

During the weeks between Purim and Passover, our lives underwent a drastic upheaval. "And there shall be no leaven, for in haste didst thou come forth out of the land of Egypt" (Deuteronomy). We had to be very careful of *chometz* (leaven) while mother watched over us as if our lives were in danger. We ate all our meals in the kitchen rather than the dining room, lest, God forbid, a breadcrumb might drop in some other part of the house and make a mysterious appearance during Passover. I shuddered to think of what heavenly judgment would have been our lot for generations to come if a single crumb had been found! Glass of all kinds had to be soaked for eight days. If mother had to *kosher* (cleanse) cutlery, it meant dropping it into boiling water which had a hot red stone in it.

Passover meant new clothes for all of us. We awakened to find them at our bedsides — new shoes, new underclothes and new dresses. Everything was so fresh and clean, and even nature gave the festival the added bonus of springtime.

One of our delights was to bring the Passover dishes, pots and pans out of the special cupboards where they had been stored all year. It was like a reunion with old friends. I invented mysterious stories about their adventures during the year. It was fortunate that no one could read my mind. My sisters, Elie and Riva, regarded me as a somewhat peculiar child. If they'd had any doubts about my sanity, my fantasies would surely have tipped the balance.

Oh, the *Seder* was so impressive! It is a domestic feast and service on the first two nights of Passover, based on actual ritual in the temple of Jerusalem. The sumptuous meal is accompanied by a running commentary of prayer, legend and exhortation, known as the *Haggadah shel Pesach*. Our table was extended, set with a white tablecloth and numerous wine cups, silver, glassware, silver candlesticks and the *matzo tash* (cover for the unleavened bread) embroidered by my mother.

A *Haggadah* was placed before each of us. A lounge chair decked with a white sheet and a large pillow on which my father reclined on his left side according to the code of Jewish law made father a king and mother his queen. During the entire week of Passover, we children were referred to as "prince" and "princess".

My father wore the ritual garment called a *kittel*, a white cotton coat which covered his *kapote*. He donned his *shtreimel*. He was every inch a king of Israel! Before we sat down, father gave us the same instruction each year: he gave us five minutes to talk, after which all our speech had to pertain to Pesach and questions about the *Haggadah*. We discussed the relationship of Passover to the concept of freedom, current events in the world and how our people were affected. We spoke about the exodus out of slavery in the land of Egypt.

The *Seder* was highlighted by the asking of the four questions, beginning, "Why is this night different from all other nights?" This honour was accorded to the youngest child; sometimes a child of only three would be called upon. This tradition assures that even young children participate in the recitation of the *Haggadah*. Jews, historically, went to great lengths and enormous expense in order to be reunited with their families on this holiday. Married children would undertake long journeys to be with their parents on Pesach.

The hiding of the *afikomen* was another of the special observances for the children. My father would break a matzo in two pieces. One, called the *afikomen*, would be hidden. While my father was somehow preoccupied, we children would seek the hidden piece of matzo, without which the service could not be completed. The child who found it would ransom it for a proper reward.

The *Seder* meal always had a special taste. Somehow the *gefilte fish*, golden chicken broth and matzo balls and roast chicken attained a new savoury flavour on the *Seder* nights. The bitter herb, symbolizing slavery, the eggs in salt water (our Red Sea) had their own sweetness on these nights. There was also the delicacy *charoses*, a mixture of apples, nuts and wine, symbolic of the bricks and mortar which the Jews were forced to build in their captivity.

Finally the moment arrived for the opening of the door to admit the prophet, Elijah. Legend has it that he is a guest at every Passover *Seder* where a glass of wine is placed for him. I always wondered how the prophet could appear in so many homes at the same time but didn't dare ask. I would walk to the door accompanied by hope and a fair measure of fear. I wondered what to do if the prophet actually appeared! Terror seized me; it was a thrilling moment. I made my way slowly, prolonging the precious moments. How would Elijah look? He would have to have a very long beard, for who could visualize such a Jew without one? He would be very old and have deep, penetrating eyes. He must have a staff; after all his walking, it would be necessary to lean on a great staff. Certainly, I thought, he must walk. No Jewish prophet could desecrate a holiday by driving!

The most solemn holiday was Rosh Hashanah, the new year, which ushers in the holy months, a time for repentance, prayer and charity. My father blew the *shofar* (ram's horn) every morning as he recited his daily prayers. It is written in the Code of Jewish Law "Shall a cornet be blown in a city, and the people not become afraid?"

Father bestowed blessings on his children, just before mother lit the candles on the Sabbath and festivals. We formed a line outside father's study and waited our turn. The eldest entered first. Father would place his hands on our heads in blessing. His face lit up, his deep eyes shone as he looked at us and uttered the benediction. There was so much love in him! He regarded each of us as an inseparable part of himself. He bent our heads and bestowed a kiss on each brow. It seemed to me as though this precious ceremony was connected to the time of our forefathers when Abraham blessed Isaac, and Isaac blessed Jacob.

Ah, those were wonderful times! It seems to me that all that pertained to Jewish life had a flavour, and so much meaning—the observance of the dietary kosher laws, the Sabbath and the festivals. Family life was sacred, and divorce a disease to be guarded against. Assimilation was unheard of, desecration of the Sabbath a crime, and marriage out of the faith was not even mentioned in a whisper.

But change was around the corner. No one mentioned the word "assimilation". Parents regarded their children as the bastions of the faith. They thought nothing would change. In Poland and Russia Jews did not fear assimilation; the Poles and Russians were the enemies. Perpetrators of pogroms, they ravaged and looted. Their hoodlums humiliated old Jews and pulled out their beards. Who then would wish to join their evil forces?

Here in Canada, God be thanked, there was freedom and peace. Children would be educated, enter professions and be good Jews. No one thought otherwise. But there was a price to pay. The first generation were immigrant children. The second generation began to perceive that here in Canada and the United States, Gentiles were not killers; they were human, benevolent. Thus assimilation began.

# CHAPTER 4

## Recollections from My Girlhood

THE FIVE YEARS WE SPENT in Toronto were very important in my development. They were coloured by two environments: school and home. As soon as we were settled in our new home, we girls were sent off to nearby McCall School. Each day I looked forward to my walk under the stately slowly turning trees on my way to school. Those years are boldly drawn in my memory — the trees, the green grass, the scent of flowers and the feeling of security.

But it was difficult for me in the beginning. I remember my first day at school. As I had a slight cold, mother wrapped a towel around my throat tied at the back. I looked exactly like what I was — a little nine-year-old immigrant girl. A loud laugh greeted my entrance to the classroom. I stood trembling at the teacher's desk, utterly humiliated. How cruel children can be! One day, the boy who sat behind me tied my long braids to the inkwell on his desk. I was unable to move and couldn't explain. Not being able to speak English was a hardship.

Another painful incident occurred when a fellow classmate mislaid a book her mother had purchased for her the previous day. She was convinced I had stolen it. True, I had been looking closely at it. Perhaps she detected longing in my eyes. She approached our teacher, insisted I stole the book and demanded its immediate return. Our teacher motioned for me to appear before her, and there I stood petrified. I had no idea what transpired, but I knew instinctively that I was in trouble. In a few moments the book was found in the owner's desk. I then realized I had been accused of stealing.

Not being capable of making myself understood spurred me on to learn the language quickly. Avidly, I began to read books on all subjects, and my thoughtful teachers encouraged me. The teachers were mostly older women and spinsters. They had a special helpful interest in their immigrant students. They must have felt their potential in molding our young lives. School was my passion, and I tried never to miss a day of classes.

The library became my personal house of worship. I persuaded my mother to let me stay for lunch at school enabling me to spend more time there. Miss Milgram, the librarian, took me in hand. She gave me a note that allowed me into the adult section of the library. I was eleven and overjoyed at being taken so seriously. She really taught me how to read using a method I still follow — to read slowly and with a dictionary. Miss Milgram said that a book was like a journey, to travel fast meant to forget where one had been. She would regard me through her glasses, which were always halfway down her nose. "Don't be so fierce," she would say. She gave me so much of herself; I owe her a lot.

There was yet another treasure trove of books! Hannah's husband was a junk dealer, and I found a mass of reading material behind her home. Books of every description! Hannah's house had a back shed, and there I would sit, unbeknownst to anyone, working my way through wonderland by the hour. Books — history, poetry, art and the English classics in the best condition! Never could I understand how anyone could have been capable of casting off my beautiful, illustrated friends.

My greatest pleasure was arriving at school early. I assisted my teacher with the correction of papers. One morning I arrived earlier than usual. I hesitated at the door of the classroom as I overheard my teacher talking, "Little Leah is coming early this morning. What a child that is! A real study in character." At the time, I did not know if that was good or bad. Perhaps it is just as well that I am still not certain.

Some of my teachers invited me to their homes. They served tea and cookies with all due respect to my observance of the kosher law. They never discriminated or condescended about my being Jewish. They offered only encouragement to go on with my education, to read and to study.

Considerable excitement centred around the debating team I was invited to join. Those debates took place in the higher classes, so my participation was arranged through the intercession of my teachers. I was so pleased and anxious not to fail that I enlisted the aid of the *shoychtim* who came weekly to our home. They acted as my opponents. The debates became so exciting that father would rush in to engineer a settlement.

I was also permitted to enter essay contests, and to the delight and indignation of my teachers, several times the essays were returned stating, "This could not have been written by a pupil."

One memorable day one of my teachers came to our home with the simple and direct purpose of encouraging my parents to send me to high school and then to university. My parents could not speak English, and the teacher's appearance caused them considerable alarm. Fortunately, an interpreter arrived and was able to translate. I was never informed by my parents of this visit, nor did they respond to it.

In those years in Toronto I did not get much attention. I was observant, quiet and studious. Father surmised that I had an aptitude for learning. He was particularly proud that I participated, albeit only by listening, in the rabbinical discussions. But he never took my schooling very seriously. It was, after all, only a secular education. In retrospect I feel that I must have resented the lack of interest in my schooling. When I became a mother, I gave my children a great deal of attention. I was determined that they would not suffer such a lack.

As an early teen-ager, I stood in awe of my father. I could have been intimidated by the honour tendered him. But I did not fear him; he was ever the loving father. We had formed a bond early in life, perhaps because father never forgot that it was he who had delivered me. I was his favourite daughter.

After father I was the first one up in the morning. Father supervised breakfast and saw to it that no food entered our mouths without the appropriate benediction. There were so many benedictions — for bread, milk, meat, fish. Father did his work well. I still recite those benedictions.

As I grew older, it became my duty to accompany my father on his way to a *bris* (circumcision). This would occur on the Sabbath. By Jewish law if a city was not surrounded by a fence, one was forbidden to carry any object on the Sabbath. Because I was not yet twelve, I was permitted to transport objects. I was a carrier, not of illness, gossip or misfortune, but of the little black bag which contained the surgical instruments.

I will always remember walking beside my father, in a great effort to keep in step with him, clutching the little black bag in my hand. I loved to watch the relatives assembled at the *bris*. It was wild! Everyone drank *shnaps*, ate *gefilte fish* and cake. No matter how poor the parents, the celebration was always so abundant that one assumed that they had suddenly come into a fortune! They laughed and sang and carried on and, of course, took very little notice of me.

One Saturday as I accompanied my father to a circumcision, I had my first encounter with anti-Semitism. Father had a long beard like all orthodox men. This made him easily recognizable as a Jew and an automatic target for Christian children who threw stones at Jews. While I watched him shield his eyes, the rage at this injustice welled up in me until I felt very close to choking.

Immigrant children were admonished by their parents not to speak to strangers. There was a peculiar reason for this. Most newcomers lived in the same neighbourhood, a little ghetto of sorts. In this area, there appeared some very unconventional "stores". They had no merchandise or wares of the usual nature. They were set up as "soul savers" and catered in conversion. Their owners invited Jewish children into the shops and began by promising all manner of goodies. I was called into such a shop many times but ignored it. Many children did not speak English very well and could easily be misled. This was one of the reasons why our parents worried and kept very close watch over us.

At home I was constantly at my mother's side, preparing for meals and for festivals. In the early mornings, mother would send me across the street on Agnes Street near University Avenue to a bakery to buy hot bagels. How delicious they were! Near the bakery was a little candy store owned and operated with love by a slightly stooped old lady with very white hair. There were candies in large glass jars to choose from and toffee apples, all for a penny. Before returning to school after lunch, I would run across, with my penny. Apart from my teachers, this was one of my earliest contacts with Gentiles.

Despite the fact that I had a passion for school, my thinking was predominantly Jewish. All my decisions and conclusions were influenced by that fact. It was as if my heritage was a painting, and I was brushed into it. I was too young to realize that my life was not going to be an easy one. I was an intense spirit; all I ever did and felt was infused with an excessiveness, a depth of feeling. Just as the Sabbath candles lit up the room, so did my soul light up from Judaism. My emotions were so involved that I felt my body would erupt from sheer joy of being Jewish. It took long before I was aware of a non-Jewish world. It was a painful process, mostly I was frightened. I had encountered anti-Semitism; it was ugly.

During our five years in Toronto, I grew up very fast. I believe my childhood and girlhood merged into one. I was an adult when I was a child — perhaps because I grew up in an adult world. Immigrant life revolved around the adults. Children were clothed, fed and sent to school. There was no talk of child psychology, diet, cholesterol and, most certainly, none of sex. All through girlhood I had few school friends my age. But I was so deeply involved in the rabbinical life that I did not feel deprived.

I also developed physically very fast. I menstruated early and became full breasted. That really upset me. I was not a pretty girl, at least not in the accepted sense. My hair was straight, my eyes severe. In plain language, I did not have a doll's face. That may have been one of the reasons why my sisters dismissed me so readily. They, by comparison, were most attractive.

What causes the disparity between children of the same origin? Of what use is it to ask that eternal question? We had the same parents, grew up in the same environment, yet what shaped our characters? What I considered beautiful and pregnant with meaning, my sisters found trivial. I revelled in being a rabbi's daughter, while my sisters abhorred it.

Life in Toronto wasn't easy for our family, but it wasn't only the poverty. The daughters of a rabbi had a particularly hard time. We seemed to be the property of the congregation. A rabbi, at that time, was entirely accountable for the behaviour and sins of his children. There were other rabbis in Toronto with grown daughters, and my sisters were often compared to them. It was their special beauty and attractiveness that made my sisters the brunt of gossip and curiosity. My parents were blind to this fact. My sisters despaired of the life that was imposed upon them. They felt confined by the rules; they longed for freedom and excitement. Their beauty and spirit gave rise to a continuous battle.

My parents came to the logical conclusion that marriage was the only solution — and soon! The girls agreed because they hoped for escape. Little did they realize that marriage can be a trap as well as an escape.

I conclude, in retrospect, that my parents had gifted children. They might have achieved much had the times and constraints of my father's profession not restricted them to very limited choices. There was always the "problem" of being born female. While sons were blessed in daylight, daughters were delegated to a shady spot in life. Girls were not educated nor were they prepared for business or any other vocation. How could my parents have failed to see the innate gifts of their daughters, and how could they have failed to develop those gifts?

My sister, Chia, was very intelligent but never quite became Canadianized. Not, that is, to the point where a young man yearning to be Canadian would find her a desirable match. Chia did not go to school in Toronto. Because she was the oldest and could not speak English, she would have been placed in a class with children much younger than herself. But how ignorant and blind some are, for Chia had so much to give. Though she did not conform to popular standards of beauty, she lit up with a radiance possessed only by a select few.

Chia met a man who, we all thought, was a desirable suitor. He was the owner of a small established business. Supposedly my parents made no effort to influence Chia. But I must admit it pleased them to think that he would be able to support Chia in comfort. How little they really knew!

The courtship of Chia took several months as the affair blew hot and cold. Chia was a daughter my parents were not anxious to lose, even though they did want to see her married. Chia simply could not make up her mind. It was her decision after all, and she finally did marry Mendel.

It is not an easy task to give an exact description of Mendel. He was an astute businessman, but he made neither friends nor acquaintances. Nor did he maintain close ties with relations. He was quite hostile to society in general. To say it mildly, he was strange.

Mendel suffered from two terrible diseases, one being jealousy, the other stinginess. I think these diseases may have been related. If Chia had a dream with a man in it, Mendel accused her of having slept with that man. Mendel loved Chia very much — he doted on her. But his love was as rare and dangerous as some exotic and poisonous weed—it suffocated the beloved. How my sister survived that union, I cannot guess. She was a devoted, faithful wife and a wonderful mother. There was little personal happiness in Chia's life, except the fulfilment of motherhood. She and Mendel had three wonderful children.

There is a theory that people are the victims of fate. In Mendel's case, it was reversed—he brutalized whatever fate was around. He purchased a home, but it was a home completely devoid of comfort. Perhaps Mendel mistakenly thought the starkness of his house would discourage company.

Chia soon became a friend to her neighbours, and how she was loved by all! She was a kind of "mother confessor" in her neighbourhood. There was one unwritten law—neighbours were only welcome to come and unburden themselves during the day when Mendel was out. Even so, it was not at all unusual for him to make a sudden mysterious appearance at odd hours.

The most peculiar fact of all—Chia loved Mendel! Even my parents could not understand this. Chia would telephone them in desperation at her wit's end. All they could do was take her and the children in for respite until she could gather her courage and return to Mendel.

An early gap grew between Chia and Elie and Riva. Chia spoke Yiddish whereas Elie and Riva concentrated on learning English. Chia read Yiddish newspapers while the younger two read movie magazines which substituted vicariously for the romance and adventure they both craved.

Elie was completely different from Chia. Her figure, face and character were absolutely lovely. Her fair skin enhanced her black hair and dark brown eyes. Elie enjoyed beauty treatments which she invented and applied herself. She would sit for hours with a magnifying glass, working away with tweezers, while lotions covered her face. All this was so unnecessary for one so naturally lovely.

A typical scene in our kitchen was mother chiding Elie's vanity while Chia and Riva chatted away with the "beautician". All through this, Elie's rituals went on without interruption. It was not long before we just took Elie's obsession for granted.

Elie was very gifted; she could paint and sew and could transform an article of clothing by simply adding embroidery here, or removing a button there. Her talent would have made her a gifted fashion designer had she been born in different times.

Elie was "keeping company" with Nachum, the son of mother's "new-found" relatives. My parents were pleased and in a few months

there was talk of marriage. When Nachum first announced his intentions, father asked him what his prospects were. Nachum said that he
was in the fur business with a concern of his own. To clarify this point:
Nachum never really stated this in his own words, he had come with
his mother, and she did the talking.

The truth finally was revealed that Nachum was a peddler with a
stand in a market. He did very well, but his mother periodically relieved
him of most of his earnings. She claimed to have a sound idea — she
was "investing" his money in furs. She hit on this ingenious method
because her daughter was engaged to a furrier in a nearby town, and
everything worked out conveniently because her son-in-law did not
visit Toronto. Nachum never saw the money or the furs, and these facts
only came to light after the wedding.

My artistic, gracious and ambitious sister, Elie, married a good but
simple man, Nachum. He tried to live up to Elie's aspirations and style.
He provided her with a good home and saw that their two children
were cared for and given an education. Fortunately, Nachum had none
of his mother's cunning, and he loved Elie dearly. Elie, however, could
never quite resign herself to having married a pushcart peddler. It hurt
her pride and robbed her of the social standing which she had enjoyed
as a rabbi's daughter. Elie was a woman of great sensibilities, and
money was not an issue to her. In later years, she surrounded herself
with the beautiful things which were necessary to satisfy her exquisite
and delicate taste.

It is surprising how people discussed Elie's marriage as though they
spoke from on high and knew all the answers. "Why does Elie look
down on Nachum? He's an honest man and earns an honest living."
Perhaps this was so, but Elie had a special sensitivity. She never let
Nachum know how she felt, and if she suffered at all from his coarse-
ness, one must take into account that she was the product of a home
where learning and knowledge were the breath of life.

Elie did not retreat into herself as a weaker person might have done.
Instead, she made it her life's ambition to see that her children were
well educated and had the best of everything. Elie and Nachum were
devoted and generous parents.

I muse over the way Elie looked on her wedding day. She walked
with her head held high and her attractiveness shone. The wedding
ceremony took place in our garden under the sky. "Thus shall thy
children be, like the stars of heaven" (Code of Jewish Law).

Riva was the real beauty of the family. Her beautiful skin and
dancing flirtatious eyes were said to resemble our grandmother. She
was practical, like mother and was a business wizard in later years.

It was difficult to cope with Riva's indomitable high spirits. She wanted to go to dances, she wanted nice clothes. She wanted and she wanted, and who could blame her? She had a real complex about hair styles and changed hers weekly. Her models for arranging her thick chestnut hair came from the movie magazines which were all the rage then. Riva would have been a fantastic actress. Even now, her obsession with hair lives on. She is still a beauty and, oh my, she still acts!

I don't think Riva knew the effect she had on Elie. She outshone Elie. She played and sported, and everyone was fair game. As my sisters matured into womanhood (which happened at an earlier age in those immigrant days) an enmity emerged between Elie and Riva. There being only a slight difference in their ages, their competitiveness increased as marriage drew closer. Their early hostility grew into an estrangement that endured throughout their lives.

Riva had become engaged while we still lived in Toronto. When father visited Montreal with the intention of moving there, he took Riva with him. She realized that Montreal gave her scope. She could be freer, less restricted and more available to opportunities than in Toronto.

This created a major problem because Riva had also made up her mind that the young man to whom she was engaged would simply not do. This meant trouble since a betrothal was very binding. When an engagement was broken, it was obligatory that both parties willingly release each other from the agreement. Riva's young man bluntly refused to dissolve the engagement. He could not be blamed — Riva was intriguing, and even her coiffures were enough to keep a man interested.

It had been a hasty engagement, and I cannot remember the prospective groom very well. I do recall father pleading with him to free Riva from her vows. The affair took on a humorous aspect. It became a melodrama which the soap operas would relish. The young man held his hand over his heart and showed father how it palpitated for Riva. There was a grate in the ceiling of my father's study which led to the room above. I must confess that I shamelessly sprawled on the floor above, my ear pressed to the grate, as father reasoned with the distraught young man.

Father left his study after hours of discussion. He turned to mother, "It seems to me that the grief-stricken young man is more concerned with the blow to his heart than with the loss of our daughter. There is only one thing to do. We must supply him with a new heart. Tomorrow, I will go to the slaughter house. There I will get the heart of a strong bull." My father, therefore, must be credited with being the first man to think of a heart transplant!

The engagement remained broken without a release. The young man did recover, and his heart was mended with another bride. We were all happy with the good news. Riva, however, was somewhat disappointed. It would have given her great satisfaction if a duel could have been fought on her behalf.

In May, 1914 my brother Isaac and his wife Vera joined us. Mother must have been dreaming when she visualized Isaac becoming a rabbi. It was as impossible as sending him to the moon. He had great talent; he was material for Hollywood but, sadly, he was born before his time. He breathed the stage, but he and his wife had a hard struggle before the stage could support them.

Isaac was often the despair of both my parents and his wife. Ah, but to know him was to love him. He possessed no false charm, but a fascinating warmth and compassion. He was capable of penetrating the minds and hearts of people. His benevolence reached out toward all who came into contact with him.

My parents were tolerant and informed on all subjects except those pertaining directly to sex. As a consequence, I knew nothing about menstruation, and it came as a complete shock. I awoke one night to find myself in a pool of blood and thought, in terror, that I was bleeding to death.

I ran a high fever and wandered out of bed. It was Isaac who heard me and came to my rescue. He was so gentle. He removed my clothes and bathed me, all the while reassuring me that my experience was an ordinary bodily function. He explained the menstruation with soothing words and rid me of my fears. I was eleven years old.

Isaac was left behind like Baruch when we came to Canada. In Poland he joined a theatre group which, oddly enough, was made up of members of rabbinical families.

Vera recounted her early life with Isaac. She described how innocent Isaac looked when she first met him. During their shared existence, it was Vera who suffered most from Isaac's generosity. They no sooner had a little money than he would manage to give it away. He was not business minded and would keep a play running for the livelihood of his employees and actors. He had an enormous capacity to earn money and a greater one to get rid of it. And Vera who loved him dearly always said, "Leah, I did not lick honey with him; it was not an easy life."

Isaac met Vera while she was a member of a troupe consisting primarily of her sister and brother-in-law. Isaac joined the small group and, for a short while, it flourished. Then Vera's sister became pregnant and died on the table of a quack who performed an abortion. Her grief-stricken husband suffered a severe nervous collapse and was committed to an institution. Real psychiatric treatment was unknown, and asylums could cause more madness than they could cure. While Vera's brother-in-law awaited medical treatment in the "hospital", a fellow inmate knifed him, and he died instantly.

Vera came from a good family, but tragedies beset her from birth. Her father had been a kind and loving man and had several children. The pictures which Vera kept showed her mother and sisters to have been quite lovely. Her mother died at the age of twenty-seven of meningitis. Vera was delivered of her when she was dying. In his grief and despair Vera's father could not bear to look at his child. As an infant she was given to a foster mother who had five children of her own. The foster mother was well paid but kept the money for her own brood. Vera survived four long, hungry years while her father naturally assumed that the ample money he regularly sent would adequately keep his child. Finally Vera's aunt paid a visit to see how the abandoned child was faring. She was horrified to see the child living in filth and sucking her thumb from hunger. She left with the little girl and a new world opened up for Vera.

The aunt lived on a small farm near a Russian village where there were few orthodox families. Vera befriended their Russian peasant neighbours and was treated like a true Russian child. She learned folk songs and dances from her girl friends, milked cows and never wore shoes, not even on the Sabbath.

Vera was twelve years old when her father married a young woman who bore him more children. Finally, he sent for Vera, and her stepmother loved all the children as though they were her own. Theirs became a happy family life.

Vera's father and family made every effort to make up for her years of being neglected. Her father hired a *melamed* who taught her Yiddish and prayers. She was a brilliant pupil who quickly added both Yiddish and Hebrew to her fluent Russian. Vera sang folk songs in all three languages. She was blessed with a beautiful voice, and the groundwork was laid for a performing career.

When she and Isaac came to stay with us in Toronto, it was extraordinary how quickly Vera learned the orthodox laws from my mother. For some time I did not know the colour of her hair because she wore a *shaytl* with a black velvet ribbon keeping it in place. She had a flair for decorum, and my parents loved her dearly.

Today my sister-in-law still tells the stories of how lovingly she was treated by my parents. If my brother uttered a harsh word to her, my parents rose to her defence. He was instantly reminded that Vera was an orphan and had come to us a stranger in a strange country.

Vera and Chia became intimate friends. They were temperamentally suited to each other; they even dressed alike. On Sunday they would go to the movies arm in arm, each wearing a straw sailor hat. Vera was an accomplished seamstress, and they both wore skirts and blouses made from fifty-cent remnants. Off they went, always chatting in Yiddish.

When Isaac arrived in Canada, father once again wanted him to give up his dream of the theatre. An actor for a son was hardly considered a proud asset to a rabbi. There was tension between the two so Isaac finally went to work in a tailor shop. Gifted Isaac was to earn the magnificent sum of three dollars a week!

In Toronto Isaac and Vera's lives merged with ours. Vera became pregnant and gave birth to a son. It was a difficult pregnancy — she was slightly built and suffered the added complication of kidney trouble. The night the child was born, the house was in a turmoil. Her labour had stretched from hours to days. We were all anxious, but it was father who stayed at Vera's side throughout, ministering to her needs and giving her the courage to fight for her life. What a battle! He suggested that Isaac don his *tallis* (prayer shawl) and pray. A little baby boy was born that dreadful night.

The child became our joy for the short period of eighteen months. He died from diphtheria. Vera became a wraith, sitting on the balcony of our home, staring tragically into space. Mercifully she gave birth, at long last, to another child. Rosanna was a rare little girl, full of all the grace of her forbearers. She reflected an innate, endearing quality which melted our hearts.

Isaac and Vera soon returned to the theatre. Isaac became the prompter in the Toronto Yiddish theatre, the Lyric, on Agnes Street which later moved to Spadina Avenue. This enabled Isaac and Vera to move out of our home to rooms on University Avenue.

Eventually Isaac was not content with being a prompter. He began writing, and his first play was produced at the Lyric. I recall that evening vividly. Vera and Chia managed to persuade mother to accompany them to the theatre. She was not told that it was the opening of Isaac's first play. During the intermission Isaac ran to mother and embraced her.

The Jewish community was divided but, in spite of this, father's reputation soon reached the far corners of Canada and the United States. He began to travel extensively to preside over *Din Torahs* (Jewish courts of settlement based on the Laws of the Torah). This was the manner by which Jews could settle disputes. Many Jews were reluctant to go to a regular court of law and resorted to this traditional hearing.

Both parties agreed beforehand that the decision of the *Din Torah* would be obeyed absolutely. Each litigant stated his case. The verdict took time as father pondered the Talmudic Laws. Father occasionally allowed me to listen to a *Din Torah* if it were a particularly unusual and interesting case. How delighted I was for this honour!

It took many years of dedicated work for father to arrange the *Din Torah* into a permanent system called *Mishput Hashalom*. This system was kept in the Jewish Community Council offices. Today, it is all more sophisticated. There are often two lawyers present as well as a rabbi. The proceedings of *Mishput Hashalom*, peaceful settlement or the verdict of peace, was the result of my father's efforts.

Father's vast Talmudic knowledge and innate sense of justice made his judgments well known and respected. He began to receive attractive offers for positions in the United States. My parents seriously considered leaving Toronto, but it was a difficult decision in spite of the obvious advantages. We had accomplished much as a family against considerable odds. Chia and Elie were wed. Isaac and his wife were about to leave for Winnipeg with little Rosanna. They had been offered work in a theatre there. Riva was engaged to be married.

Mother and father finally decided that father should accept a position in the United States. Father left to sign the contract for several years. He returned to assist with the move — a fatal error! One would have thought a volcano had errupted, or a cyclone had struck our city. The Jewish community in which father had served gathered outside our house. Not one of us was allowed to leave. They said that blood would be shed in the city if father departed. We stayed, but only for a brief time.

The next offer father accepted. He came home quietly to discuss it with mother and when they had agreed, father simply left for Montreal and did not return. We were to pack and join him.

The night we left our home was filled with crying well-wishers. Men, women and children wept at our departure. It was a sad farewell for all the family.

Off we went to begin a new life. We had survived a strenuous period of adjustment in a new country. Even freedom takes time to get accustomed to. We took to heart the message of our Prophet, Jeremiah, "Seek the welfare of the country wherein ye dwell and pray unto the Lord for it; in its welfare shall be your peace!" *(Haftorah Mattos)*.

My parents, Riva, my younger brother Israel and I left for our new home. It was the year 1919.

# PART THREE

CHAPTER 5

## Our New Home
## in
## Montreal

A COLD WINTRY DAY greeted us on arrival in Montreal. Unlike Toronto, the snow stayed on the sidewalks, and the pavements became icy and difficult to navigate. Father had prepared a three-storey house for us on what was then known as Cadieux Street, later De Bullion Street. At that time, it was considered an attractive residential neighbourhood. The Jewish library was housed in a small cottage nearby.

On every street including ours there was a little grocery store. Supermarkets had not yet appeared, and it was some years before Mrs. Steinberg opened her first grocery store on "the Main" near Mount Royal Boulevard. These small shops were usually run by a married couple with occasional help from their children. They were more than just groceries stores — they were institutions. It was here that problems and the welfare of neighbours were discussed, examined and sometimes solved. They were convenient places to trade recipes which were generously shared amongst customers and proprietors. Ingredients were described so eloquently that writing them down was unnecessary. Remedies for ailments were prescribed free of charge.

We were immediately conscious of differences between Montreal and Toronto. Montreal was a far more cosmopolitan city. In general Montreal Jews came from larger European cities and already had a more sophisticated business and educational background. They were highly motivated and became prosperous more quickly than Toronto Jews who were still straining to acquire even a modest livelihood at that time. But there was a warmth and congeniality amongst Toronto Jews that I missed terribly in the more polished, restrained Montreal Jewish environment. Toronto Jews were also hard workers and ever on the lookout for *gesheft* (business), but somehow for them progress was mixed with more feeling.

When we left Toronto in 1919, I was fourteen years old. I still had two more years of public school in Montreal. Due to the attention given me so generously by my Toronto teachers, I was already advanced beyond public school in my studies. I read a lot and loved to write. School was not the same for me in Montreal. I never developed attachments to teachers similar to those I had enjoyed in Toronto, nor did I receive the same kind of support.

Aberdeen School in Montreal was remote and unfamiliar. I was also severely handicapped by my ignorance of the French language, which had not been taught in Toronto. I had longed for a scholarship which would have given me access to high school, but because of my lack of French, I did not qualify. I cried in despair.

I often wondered whether my parents would have allowed me to further my education, if I had won the scholarship. Though they knew of my disappointment, they never suggested that I continue with high school, in spite of my obvious ability and interest. When I graduated from public school with high marks, I wanted desperately to continue my schooling, but my parents decided otherwise.

I bear my father great love. However, I will never understand how a man of my father's stature and intense belief in knowledge, could have deprived me so. Nor will I ever exonerate him. Most of my struggles in my adult years, I attribute to my lack of an education that would have enabled me to earn a livelihood. I believe I could have done much with an education.

But my parents were immigrants and came from a world of persecution and pogroms brought on them by the *goyim* (non-Jews). As a result they were constantly apprehensive of all *goyim*, and thus anything secular was held suspect. During my school years, my parents were still in the throes of this kind of fear and prejudice. In a sense, they felt they were protecting me rather than depriving me by not allowing me to continue school.

There was also the fact that in my parents' time girls were simply not educated. Schooling was for boys. Sons would have to support the daughters who were brought up just for one purpose — marriage. No one thought of divorce, for marriage was forever, no matter what that marriage would entail.

After the Sabbath father, mother and I would often discuss the lecture my father had given to his congregation that morning. Always father took me to task. "Now, Leah, let me see if you understand what I spoke about." Not only did I recall what he had said, to indicate to him that I grasped the meaning, but I asked questions. Father would be thrilled and always made the same remark to mother, indicating that she was at fault, "*Nu*, why wasn't Leah born a boy?"

Father had originally come to Montreal for a *Din Torah*. A serious dispute had arisen between a powerful rabbi and a group of *shoychtim*. The upshot was that the *shoychtim* were divided into two camps. Since all *shoychtim* had to be represented and supervised by a rabbi, after the *Din Torah* father became the rabbi of those *shoychtim* whom he thought had been maligned.

The arguments in the community because of this dispute were bitter, but they did not harm father or affect our living conditions. Though the number of wealthy, influential Jews in his following could be counted on father's one hand, he received a large following in the community including several synagogues. No longer was he the rabbi of only the *Polishe*; he was proud to administer to the needs of many. I can recall the times we would enter a crowded room and all would rise to pay tribute to his eminence.

Once father was a guest at a banquet. He was seated next to one of the wealthiest Jews in Montreal, a pillar of the community. This gentleman came to father and asked, "Rabbi, if I get close to you, will some of your fame as a scholar rub off on me?" Father turned to him with a smile, "If you come close to me, I will have a greater chance of becoming a rich man than you will have of becoming a Talmudist!"

There were quite a number of rabbis in Montreal. Every Saturday night after the Sabbath, the rabbis congregated in our home. They brought their burdens to father, and he always tried to help. Rabbinical meetings pertaining to the *kashrut* (Kosher Laws) and community affairs were often held at our house as well.

In Montreal father was no longer obliged to perform circumcisions. Instead he devoted his time to *kashrut*. He was to oversee that the laws governing slaughter were obeyed by the butchers. He examined the knives for sharpness and flawlessness, ensuring no suffering to the animals. The Jewish method of slaughter causes maximum effusion of blood and instant death of the animal and is called *shechita*.

Father often took me on his tour of the slaughter house. He jokingly told mother that he was training me to be the first woman rabbi. When father told mother that I was to go with him, she protested. "I think it will be too much for her. She may get frightened by the animals and the huge knives." But father insisted I had to become acquainted with the *shechita*. And so I did.

In those years, *kashrut* played an important part in Jewish homes. Chickens were purchased live and slaughtered right in the chicken store. The chicken was opened by the housewife and inspected to see if there was a pin or needle lodged somewhere which would make the chicken *trayf* (non-kosher). If this was the case, the fowl was brought to father. Thursday was the busiest day, for the chickens were prepared for the approaching Sabbath. I was the one who brought the chickens to father to examine. I would stand by, watching father at work.

Soon father began to initiate me. He would examine the chicken, look at me and say, "*Nu*, Leah, kosher or *trayf*?" Certainly he did not rely on my judgment, but I managed to master the chickens much to father's delight.

We always lived in a house with very few stairs for my parents to climb up from the street. Once father heard someone at the door. He opened it and discovered a huge dog ensconced in the front hall. Father, who loved all animals, politely asked the dog to leave. The dog refused to obey. He just lay there in a dejected pose and stared at father with two soulful eyes. Father decided that the dog had the soul of a non-kosher butcher and had come to beg his forgiveness. He turned to the dog and said, "*Kalef* (dog), I will open the door so that you can walk out. I see by your demeanour that you are the soul of Zalman, the butcher, who disobeyed the law." Father's eyes twinkled. "You see, what you did was an unforgivable misdeed." Father stroked his beard and paused, "I forgive you. Go, and rest in peace." Believe it or not, the dog got up and walked out.

It is not clear to me at what age my father began his career as a writer. He spoke Russian and Polish fluently, and satisfied his appetite for knowledge by studying history, the great thinkers of the day and the new discoveries in science and medicine. Nothing of interest escaped his scrutiny, and our household subscribed to newspapers from many countries. Constantly he added to hisvvast collection of rare *sphorim*.

Father wrote sermons, interpretations of the Bible and the Talmud, stories and poetry. It was a standing joke in our family that, when mother needed money for a forthcoming festival, father would just write another book.

My father's greatest gift to Jewish thinkers was his translation of the *Zohar*. It took my father twenty-five years to translate the *Zohar* from the original Aramaic into Hebrew. It was handwritten in beautiful script with a quill pen, which father had made. There was a soft sound to that pen, music that still reverberates in my very being. Through the years as I watched father write, it seems I breathed with each stroke of that pen.

The *Zohar* was composed by Moses de Leon in the thirteenth century and attributed to Shimen Ben Yechui of the second century. It is a mystical, symbolic interpretation of Jewish writings and Law, and is studied in most Jewish houses of learning. The *Zohar* can be found in a facsimile of my father's script as well as in reproduction at libraries and synagogues all over the world. While the *Talmud*, a collection of Jewish civil law and religious law, demands a precise, informative mind, the *Zohar* appeals more to the heart. It expands upon and sometimes contradicts the straightforward practical rationalism of the Talmudic tradition. Its main thrust is the relationship of God and man.

Our lives to a great extent revolved around my father's work on the translation of the *Zohar*. Those twenty-five years affected all the members of our family. We must have been deprived of many important things. All available funds as well as private donations were directed towards the publication. Supplies and money were sent to the typesetter in Warsaw, Poland.

When Father had completed his writing for the day, I would sit on the little stool where he rested his feet. His image was serious as he spoke to me. "Leah, it is good to contemplate all aspects of life. I want you to have an understanding of *Cabala*. It will enrich your existence." Father would stroke my head as he spoke. He described the splendours of heaven, and the glory of the life hereafter, in terms of mysticism.

Later in life, my avid reading exposed me to great thinkers. While those helped to shape my mind, they never really altered it. Father had inculcated me with the doctrine of the *Zohar*, *Cabala* and Chassidism which were written on my soul with indelible ink that could never be erased.

Sometimes my attitude towards my father's work was not as magnanimous. In his arduous work of translating the *Zohar*, father derived great pleasure when one of the volumes arrived. It was a spiritual achievement and called for a celebration. We sat together, and father clasped the book to his chest. "Leah, this work is part of me. It is almost like a child of mine. It will live." Somehow I found that extremely upsetting and said, "Father you have fulfilled yourself to a great extent in your Talmudic works. But it is through your children, your descendants, that your memory and greatness will live. Through them generations will go on and on, for it is they who will carry on the heritage."

Father rose, his face suffused with anger. "Leah, you dare speak thus to your father. It seems to me you have forgotten that I am your father." He hurriedly left the room. We did not speak to each other for several days.

Mother also listened as father admitted us to the realm of *Cabala*. Referring to an aspect of the afterlife, he said that if a man were married twice, it was ordained in heaven that he spend there the same number of years with each wife as he had spent in this world. This naturally upset mother as she was unwilling to share father at all, and was secretly afraid that the period of seven years — the duration of father's first marriage — might somehow be prolonged. Perhaps it is coincidence, still it is fact, that my mother was incurably ill for seven years and died at the end of that time. I fervently pray that they are together now.

When father made a special prayer book for me, he wrote a specific name for me in Hebrew on its cover. I asked the reason behind this name which bore no resemblance to my own. He assured me that it was my true name. When life ceased for us, he explained, and we entered the true world, an angel approached and asked our name. "Just suppose," I queried, "that I forget my special name." He reassured me that once I had memorized the name, it would remain steadfastly in my memory. So important are childhood teachings that I still have my father's prayer book, and in it is that special name.

Notwithstanding the changes for the better that our move from Toronto to Montreal brought about, the life of a rabbi was still not an easy one. For years, rabbis were sustained mainly by the synagogues they served. They received a minimum stipend, which was insufficient and seldom paid regularly. For years the rabbis had been agitating and organizing with the purpose of forming a Jewish Community Council and a Rabbinical Council. The Community Council was to pay salaries to the rabbis, providing them with a proper livelihood at last. But in order to achieve this increase in salary, a tax would have to be paid on kosher meat. Members of the Jewish community protested against the higher prices of meat, and the rabbis were accused of greed.

We became victims. Just before Yom Kippur a crowd gathered outside our home and threw stones. Father finally went out and faced the people. He told them their behaviour was unforgivable and not to be taken lightly a day before Yom Kippur. The people were petrified and left.

Finally the battle was won. The Jewish Community Council and Rabbinical Council came into being. Salaries were settled, and the rabbinical profession became an honourable one at last.

Riva and my father had gone to Montreal before mother, Israel and I. While she waited for us to join them, Riva met Mark. He came from a good, well-established family and owned a thriving business. The new reality of cosmopolitan Montreal stirred something in Riva which small-town Toronto had left unawakened. She enjoyed a new freedom, a new world and a satisfying release. Flattery and compliments went to her head. Her marraige to Mark was strongly opposed by my parents, for he was twenty years older than Riva. They tried to explain to Riva what such a great difference in their ages could mean to her life.

Mark owned a car, and Riva called me outside to see it, giving me the dubious honour of being taken for a ride. I watched her smooth her hand over the back seat of the car. She caressed the upholstery with a sensuous touch. She loved that car and cherished it, almost as if it were alive.

Riva and Mark were married in 1920. Before the ceremony, my parents talked to Riva in a little anteroom of the synagogue pleading with her not to go through with the wedding. They told her that, although the reception had been arranged, it would make no difference to them, and that they would bear the consequences. But they were married — Riva and this older man.

The arrival of my eldest brother Daniel and his family presented yet another problem for us. His was a large family, he had no trade and lacked an aptitude for study. Father began to teach him the profession of ritual slaughterer and before long he became quite successful. We were relieved when he was able to move his family and possessions into their own home. His wife Rivka never got along with mother. Perhaps they were too close in age.

When Sander arrived, the problem arose of finding a profession for him. Father gave Sander financial aid to support his family in another house and began training him for the rabbinate. Since Sander was already well versed in the Torah, it did not take him long to receive *smicha* and became a rabbi. After due deliberation father concluded that it would be best for Sander to seek a position in the United States. Small towns in Canada employed a rabbi who filled in as *melamed*; in the United States, there were congregations capable of supporting a full-fledged rabbi. Father sent advertisements to the Yiddish newspapers. Sander had the minor drawback of a limited English vocabulary, but years ago in the Jewish community even children were fluent in Yiddish. I visited him daily to talk to him in English and became his guide.

Ultimately Sander secured a position in the United States, and our trials concerning his visa began. He and I went to the American consulate each day — a weary and fruitless effort. The employees at the embassy seemed to have been hired for the sole purpose of preventing us from seeing the consul. One day our number was finally called. A woman questioned us, and we were welcomed into the consul's office.

Sander stood near a filing cabinet and never uttered a word. It was left to me to tell the whole story beginning with Sander's immigration, his family, what the position would mean to him — to us. The consul listened. I seemed to rave on and on and, finally, petered out. The consul raised his hand and said gently, "It's all right, little lady, your brother will get the visa." And he did! Sander and I did not walk, we flew out of the office. Soon after, he and his family left Montreal.

After that episode at the consulate, I became the official procurer of visas. I met the demands of relatives, friends and near kin who claimed my father's hospitality and my help.

This caravan of long lost and sometimes mysterious relatives continued for years. Those on their way to the United States awaited visas. They spoke no English and had to be accompanied to the American embassy. There was no competition for the job of errand runner. I achieved my position of translator and visa procurer by popular acclaim. Many and varied were my sufferings amid the sad and ridiculous situations which developed around my new post. I doubted the sanity of these "relatives" and feared for my own.

In addition to myself, there was another "independent agent", a well-educated older man. He was simply a good person whose aim in life was to assist fellow human beings in need. He came to the immigration office whenever he had time to help the new immigrants. We met there often and were subject to the same treatment. We were both humiliated, frustrated and often literally thrown out of the office.

At one point I was trying to procure a visa for my Uncle Reuben. The office was jammed with people seeking to get visas. All had numbers, and all had been waiting for a long while. Someone with a lower number pushed ahead of us, and I protested. I should have known better. The officer in charge, a tall dark man resembling a Russian Cossack, held me up to ridicule. I was so tired of the whole visa business that I was on the verge of tears.

The officer finally took us before the other petitioners. Then, the inquisition began. "Under what category did your uncle wish to enter the United States?" I answered "rabbinical", because it was the easiest visa to procure. Then Uncle Reuben was asked for his passport, and that did it! The passport had my uncle listed as a merchant. The officer glared at me and demanded why the passport said "merchant" and not "rabbi". I honestly do not know how I found the courage to invent this reply. I explained how difficult it was in Poland to make changes in a passport. My uncle had, indeed, been a merchant but, since the war, he could not earn a living in that capacity. He was well versed in the Torah and had, naturally, turned to the rabbinate. Furthermore, I stated with some vehemence, my uncle was so learned that he could have, if he had so wished, achieved a rabbinical diploma.

There was a long silence as the immigration officer thoughtfully looked at me and smiled. I thought I was in serious trouble, and I was not sure what his smile meant. He left the room and later returned with another official. "Take a good look at this young woman. I asked her a question and this is how she answered." He repeated my little story and asked if his colleague could have made a better reply. They decided no, no one could have. I was overjoyed.

We succeeded in getting the visa and, as we were leaving, the tall dark officer followed and asked us to enter another office. He apologized for his rude behaviour and invited me to sit with him the next day to witness another day of immigration dilemmas. Then he said, "Please, I want you to know that I am a Jew. You cannot possibly appreciate the position in which I find myself. I want to help, but being Jewish renders me impotent. I raise my voice to ease my pain. I must perform strictly as an officer, all the more so because I am a Jew."

The next day I returned to sit at a desk beside the Jewish officer. I found my friend, the kindly man who led the immigrants by the hand. We sat together for the better part of that sad day. Some of the applicants wanted to emigrate permanently, others wished to acquire visas for visits only. There was one elderly orthodox lady with a *shaytl* and an impatient daughter-in-law. "How old are you?" asked the officer. This was dutifully translated from the Yiddish by the daughter-in-law. Answer: "Tell him it is not his business." Next question: "How much money are you taking with you?" Yiddish again: "I told you he looks like a thief." Question: "How long will you stay in New York?" The reply: "Do I know if I can stand Chanah Bashe for more than a week?" Well, life certainly did have its lighter moments.

I also become something of a fixture at Canadian customs. Father's books were typeset in Warsaw and printed in Canada, and it was always my duty to pick up the plates. My mother wore a *shaytl*, the custom for orthodox women. Mother's was imported from Poland as they were a very rare commodity in Canada in those days. This invaluable article had to be reclaimed at customs, and I was the delegate. I, a little figure, stood at the wicket considering how on earth one explained wigs. I was shy and embarrassed. Who would believe the custom of cutting off a bride's hair and, alas, I had to convince them that the wig was a religious object and as such was duty free. The customs inspector was amused and smiled whenever he saw me and cheerfully handed over all packages addressed to father. That rescued me when I went to retrieve the wigs. The greeting was, "What have we got for the rabbi's little daughter today?" Someone kind must have watched over wig redeemers!

Montreal wrought many changes, particularly in my relationship with my father. Father was much more content. All of his daughters except me were married, and Isaac was well on his way to success. Thus, he was able to devote more of his time to Israel and me.

Father's life was so constituted that he was obliged to rely on others for his commercial transactions. He did not speak English and could not spare the time to do simple chores because of his community responsibilities and his writing. Also he was the focus of unwelcome attention in the streets because of his Chassidic garb. Thus he never entered a shop or visited a theatre or concert hall, nor was he likely to go to a post office or bank. A barber and a tailor came to our home regularly. Medical checkups were done at home.

Father needed someone to do his errands. What began with simple tasks, soon evolved into much more. Gradually I became father's *shammes* — his messenger and his confidante. I was able to help him to write letters and make telephone calls. Father's slogan became, "I will send Leah."

Each new duty I was assigned brought me closer to father. And although I was still an adolescent, father soon ceased to treat me as one. He had the utmost trust in me, and what gave me so much pleasure was that he consulted me as to which course I should pursue when he sent me on an errand. I believe there was a strong affinity between father and myself. Several times he told me, "You are my child Leah, but you are not like any of my other children."

After I left school, I became part of the rabbinical routine. I was in father's office often to interpret in English for him. There I had ample opportunity to watch and learn. Father confided in me and discussed problems involved in counselling and guidance. I was intrigued. That too became part of my education.

My activity in the rabbinical life never ceased while my father was alive. It grew with the years and sharpened my mind. It developed me in ways that served me later in life to think, to weigh matters and have faith in myself. It became the sustaining force in my life—as an adolescent, as an adult, as a wife and mother. Often in my mind I traced the times with father, and I thought if father relied on me, I can rely on myself.

# CHAPTER 6

## People
## and
## Letters

WITH SWEET NOSTALGIA, my mind goes back to the characters who frequented our home — people who came to escape the cold and to bathe themselves in the warm glow cast by my parents.

It was father's dubious honour to receive Gimple. Tall, gaunt, oddly dressed, with a voice that carried and a wisp of a beard, Gimple thought he was the messiah. He assured father that he had been sent directly from heaven with no stopovers. His mission was that he pursue his messianic destiny and put it into effect and, to this end, Gimple devised a program.

RULE 1: Jews had to fast one day a week.

RULE 2: A certain percentage of their earnings was to be donated to charity and Gimple, himself, would attend to this.

RULE 3: The Sabbath was to be observed without reservation, and only Yiddish was to be spoken on that day.

RULE 4: Every bride was to have her hair cut before the wedding and observe the *Mikva* Law.

I always entertained the eerie sensation that Gimple wanted to supervise the last rule personally.

One really had to see Gimple in action. He would rise to his full height and begin to tell us how he heard a voice telling him that he was the real messiah—not an imitation. He was commanded to devise a plan which would lead the Jews he failed to say where, and a new era would begin. His speech never varied nor did his style, but as Gimple said, "Why change a good thing?"

Gimple was a divorced man. Father admonished him, "How can a religious Jew claim to be the messiah when he has no wife?" Gimple agreed that father was right and told him that father should find a wife for him. Father said that it would be a *mitza*, but he could not decide for whom.

Then came Rab Itshe Meyer. He would appear periodically after Purim. He had a very serious problem. An old man, leaning on his cane, wearing a mournful look, he began, "*Rebbe*, what about my dentures? I cannot ask my children to buy new ones to use for Passover and, if they did, should I not require two sets, one for dairy and one for meat? And how can I dispense with my dentures and eat the hard matzos?"

Father's reply never varied, "Rab Itshe Meyer, I must give this matter deep thought." Out came the Code of Jewish Law while Rab Itshe Meyer waited in hushed anticipation. Then, "I have arrived at a decision. You will remove your dentures for one day before the festival, place them in a solution of salt water and do likewise after eating meat, leaving your dentures in the water for six hours, after which, you may eat dairy." Rab Itshe Meyer sighed with relief.

As the characters who enjoyed the hospitality of our home pass before me, I try to breathe life into them with the hope that, whoever reads these pages, may reap from them the same delight that I did.

May I introduce to you, Rab Feivish, the *shadchen*? Always in a hurry, his haste made him stutter as he tried to impart his messages as fast as possible in order to achieve results in the same way. Father said that he reminded him of the merchant who had no wares of consequence to sell, so he was always running. When the merchant was asked, "Why are you running?" his reply was, "So that people will think I am in business."

Rab Feivish was a short, thin man. I was constantly afraid the wind would blow him away. His beard was also thin. On a windy day his beard would be held aloft as if on wires. I worried that it might not come down again. His eyes always held a questioning look. He was ever on the alert for parents with sons and daughters of marriageable age. That meant business.

Rab Feivish plied his trade with pictures. He had dozens of them which he placed in two upper pockets of his coat. It was not an ordinary suit, nor did he dress in the garb of a Chassid. He was what you might call an "in between" Jew. After all, he did have to consider his livelihood. He catered to both Chassidim and *mitnagdim* alike. Business was business! His jacket was three-quarter length and from his black hat protruded his velvet skull cap. He would remove his hat and wipe the perspiration from it. I always wanted to ask why he wiped his hat but not his head. However, that was not a proper question to ask.

Those photographs served a purpose. The males resided in one pocket, the females in another. They must not touch, God forbid! In order to demonstrate his merchandise, Rab Feivish had to put on his glasses; later he removed them. That was how the calamity befell. When he replaced the pictures without his glasses, he put the males in the same pocket as the females and, if that were not catastrophic enough, he had placed the males on top of the females!

Rab Feivish did not take such incidents lightly. In such cases he would run to father to confess his "sin". At first, father pointed out that the pictures were merely paper, which only made matters worse. So father agreed with Rab Feivish that it was of grave importance. Out came the *Mishnah* and the Code of Jewish Law. Father leaned over the *sphorim*. Finally, he turned to the *shadchen*, "Rab Feivish, it was a sin to place the pictures in so tempting a manner. When that happens again, God forbid, you will be obliged to fast two half days a week." This placated Rab Feivish — he would be able to atone for his sins.

Shmarye, the *melamed*, came to call on mother. Shmarye and his older daughter ran a *cheder* in their home. The *melamed* had been searching for a wife for a year. He had a sad history with wives — two had deserted him, having run off with other men. Tense situations came and went with the search for a wife. Candidates for the heart of Shmarye met with drastic treatment.

He would turn up and give mother a vivid description of the aspirant. If the lady appeared promising, Shmarye would disappear for a month. When he returned, it was always the same sad lament. He had entertained a visitor from the other world, in this case his brother, may he rest in peace. And this dead brother divulged the terrible secret that the lady he had been seeing was a divorcée. And the *melamed* was a *Kohen* which meant that he was not permitted to marry a divorced woman. Each woman Shmarye courted suffered the same fate thanks to another departed relative. The process seemed endless, for Shmarye was blessed with many deceased relations.

Mother appealed to father for advice. He told her that Shmarye had two paths to follow. First, to get a list of all his departed relatives and address them one by one. Second, as soon as a relative appeared, to threaten each that he or she would have to be buried once more. And that was the eventual cure.

There was also Rab Gershon, the *shister* (shoemaker). His insistence on that full title took over an hour's explanation with gesticulations and time off for some prayers. It was no easy task to clarify what Rab Gershon actually meant. Also it was not unusual for Rab Gershon to change his mind right in the middle of his reasoning.

After tugging furiously at his beard and using the Talmudic sing-song, Rab Gershon confided to father that he was a prophet. He had to hide his true identity in the guise of a labourer just as the great sages of biblical times had done. It was a secret between himself and God.

There was, however, a slight problem. He was unable to decide which prophet he was. Various great ones like Isaiah, Jeremiah, Elijah would come to him in dreams and the choice was still to be made. Could father help him? Father told him the world had been waiting many years for a messiah. They would have to wait also for Rab Gershon to decide which prophet he chose to be.

One man I sincerely liked was Getzel, the *bucher* (bachelor). It was a joy to listen to his system. It was a way of life he discovered all by himself. His power lay in the fact that he was a bachelor with a nice business. Since there were many girls of marriageable age, mothers from everywhere vied for Getzel and the competition was keen. Getzel thrived on that and so did his stomach.

Through Rab Feivish, the *shadchen*, Getzel arranged for meetings with prospective families. These always took place at their dinner tables. Sumptuous were the meals that were served to our hero. Usually, he would contrive to appear on the Sabbath. He was mad about *tsholent*, a casserole of potatoes, meat and beans that was kept on a low flame throughout the Sabbath.

The set-up was perfect. Getzel would visit each prospect twice, then on to the next victim. Getzel had two worries. One, that another *bucher* would learn this tactics and usurp his territory; the other, that time would exhaust his resources.

One of the duties of a rabbi during those years was that of a marriage counsellor. Many couples came for help. At least one of these appeared monthly, regular as the tick of a clock. Father referred to them as *und yener* (and the other man?).

In such cases the jealous husband usually accused his wife of having a lover. For a realistic onlooker, one look at the wife would immediately dispel that notion. Normally, it took father two hours to make peace between the two — the husband agreeing that he was foolishly suspicious. He promised never again to nourish such an idea. He would then walk his wife to the door, turn to father and, forgetting all that father had said, would ask again, "So, *rebbe, und yener?*"

Often, members of the so-called "first families" of the community would arrive with marriage problems, children difficulties, various troubles that raged and intensified for many reasons. It was like tangles with knots. We were often shocked by what we heard, not because the elite faced diversity, but how they reacted to those circumstances. Consequently, it was incredible to watch the same people at communal affairs. There, they were soft spoken, polite and dignified. How devastated they would have been had I inquired about the progress of their grievances!

One of the most delightful people we entertained was the eminent cantor, Yosele Rosenblatt. His records are treasures today. His stay in our home was a pleasure. This charming human being entertained us with anecdotes of his extensive travels. A cantor who loved his work, he was well learned and, therefore, contributed great depth to the services and prayers. It can be truthfully said that his equal does not exist today.

Shimshen Hagiber, Samson the strong, tall, handsome and vibrant, was a widower with one daughter, Zipporah. She kept house and taught the elementary classes. The *cheder* was in their home. Everyone strived to earn their living within the confines of their own home if at all possible. Shimshen and his daughter were inseparable. Although Zipporah was well into her twenties, any mention of her marriageable age was dismissed by her father.

As father was removing his phylacteries after morning prayers, Zipporah suddenly appeared looking distraught and tearful. She wanted to see father alone. Father readily found time and came from his study to comfort her. After deliberation, he took me by the shoulders, his hands trembling, "Hurry, Leah, hurry! Call Brina, and ask if she has a vacant room." That accomplished, I was asked to take Zipporah home, pack her belongings and escort her to Brina's.

When it was over, father told us that Zipporah had suffered her father's unnatural sexual advances for some time. She had pretended not to understand. When this performance reached what she realized to be a dangerous stage, she ran to father for help. Incest was unheard of. We had thought it was impossible.

We often hosted *oyrechim*. Mostly, these were men who travelled as fund raisers for Hebrew schools, old age homes and *yeshivas*, or such institutions which were in need of financial support. Sometimes *oyrechim* would include a rabbi applying for a position, or a cantor in need of one. They never had any money, but we were fortunate— they never imposed their speeches or prayers on us.

My parents keenly felt their separation from Chia and Elie who had stayed in Toronto. Mother often went to visit, taking Israel with her and leaving me with father to keep house. One morning when mother was away, I answered the door to find a disreputable-looking middle-aged man. At that time, begging was an honourable profession. He said that he was hungry. I asked him in, fed him a hot meal and sent him on his way with a bountiful supply of sandwiches. Father in his *tallis* was reciting his morning prayers when he saw this departure from his window. He came into the kitchen where I was sitting innocently eating breakfast and proceeded to admonish me for admitting a stranger into the house when I was alone. He warned me that such men were unsavoury and a risk.

Two days after this incident, toward evening, father went to the door and admitted two men into the house. He asked me for blankets and linens and then proceeded to make a bed for them. He explained to me that they were hungry and penniless. They stayed for two days. The day following their leaving, I felt that father was keeping an anxious eye on me. He looked at me and turned quickly away when I returned his gaze. Another day passed, and I kept wondering why I itched so. Eventually, father asked, "Leah, do I see a red spot on your arm?"

"Really, father, I don't know about my arm," I admitted, "but I do know that I itch all over!" Father confessed that he itched also. He sent me to the pharmacy for a salve and advised me to bathe immediately. It took us three days to get deloused!

I planned my revenge. So *I* was not to admit strangers! I calmly approached father and asked for a new dress. It wasn't an easy thing to do, and father made excuses. "Father," I casually stated, "I wonder whether I should telephone mother, or wait for her return, to tell her about our two 'licey' guests."

"Blackmail!" he accused. "Could you blackmail your own father?" I remained calm, replying, "Surely you don't expect me to blackmail a stranger? That would be dangerous." I was given the money for my new dress, and father got tea with lemon.

Our guest room was seldom vacant. One afternoon, a *rebbe*, who was a *tzaddik* (a self-proclaimed miracle worker) descended on us with three suitcases — always a bad sign. Behind him followed, not only his holy shadow, but also the *rebbetzin* (*rebbe's wife*). They were both breathless. My mother was in the habit of serving food when *oyrechim* arrived, but on this occasion she did not make any effort. Father recognized the signs of a battle and retreated from the war zone, while I stayed to watch with anticipation.

Mother began by inviting the two guests to sit down. She began her strategy in dulcet tones — always a dangerous sign. "Worthy *rebbetzin*, we have much in common. You are the wife of a *rebbe*, and much honour is due you. I am the wife of a rabbi, and much honour is due me. Therefore, we have this one small problem. Who, I ask, shall wait on whom?" Out they went, suitcases and all!

Father's reputation, as a family counsellor spread to distant areas. Mail arrived from places we had never heard of, due in part to father's books which had made their way into Jewish bookshops around the world. Most letters were written in Yiddish, but they were soon followed by letters in English, which I was honoured to translate.

Father never mastered the English language, and it was a standing joke between us that I would teach him to become fluent in English. We set aside one day each week, when I would answer his questions in English. It was hopeless. English was tongue-twisting to father. Then, mother joined us, and it ended as fun sessions.

Poignant appeals for help were common. I recall vividly a letter from Australia. It was from a woman of forty who was having an affair with her boss. She was unmarried and sexually starved, and after twelve years of employment she finally appealed to this gentleman to enter into a sexual relationship with her. At first he declined this kind invitation. He was happily married, but as she admitted, she pursued him relentlessly. He finally agreed. The affair lasted five years before he called a halt. He did not want to lose his wife. The correspondent wanted to know if she had the right to feel that the man owed her an obligation to continue the intimacy between them.

Father's reply was an emphatic "no". He was gently understanding and told her that she need not harbour shame or remorse for her sexual needs, but was to leave her job immediately.

The reply to Australia dispatched, I said. "Father, I have conceived a bright idea." Father responded with mock alarm, "Well, *Talmud kop* (wise head), what now?"

"It is time society recognized the plight of unmarried women and their need for sex. Therefore, funds should be allocated for a benevolent institution that would have a supply of males ready to volunteer, out of the goodness of their hearts, to oblige these frustrated females. And since such a lofty undertaking would require the services of a supervisor, I nominate myself for that post."

Mother gave father a look. She said, "And you wanted her to be a rabbi?"

A disturbing letter arrived from a small town in Texas. It contained an outline of an intrigue that had the earmarks of a mystery bestseller. Included in the letter were signatures of business and professional men testifying to the validity of its contents. There was also a plea from the rabbi of the town, who frankly stated that he was unable to settle the serious dispute. The author of the letter, a young man in his early thirties called Leibish Shtern, pleaded for help.

Leibish had become betrothed to a girl, Dinah. She was the second of three daughters of a well-to-do family. The three girls were slightly over a year apart in age. That accounted for the fact that Leibish Shtern had taken out all three sisters separately and then concentrated his attentions on Dinah. Later they became engaged. Shortly after, Leibish sensed a coolness from the family directed at him and Dinah, followed by stark hostility.

Leibish was the son of orthodox parents, so the following events proved to be a terrible shock. Arriving home, he was accosted by his parents who were very upset, to say the least. They revealed to their son that Dinah's parents had just left their home. During their visit, they had disclosed these awesome facts. Dinah was not really their daughter. She was a *shiksa* (Gentile woman), the illegitimate child of a Polish mother and father. It had happened on board a ship from Poland. Among the passengers were a Jewish couple with one child, a baby girl, another young woman alone with a tiny baby girl. The young mother died on board ship. The Jewish couple with the little girl took the dead mother's baby with them to Texas. It was as simple as that.

They reared the little girl they named Dinah as their own. She never knew otherwise. Neither the history of her unfortunate mother nor her adoption were divulged to her until she became engaged.

On the advice of my father, Leibish, his parents and Dinah came to Montreal. Dinah was tall, willowly and blond with blue eyes and a straightforward expression. Speaking Yiddish well, her hands gesturing to emphasize all she said, she kept repeating, "Rabbi, I am a Jewish daughter. I do not know anything else."

There was no doubt that Dinah had been brought up with love in the same manner as her sisters. What, then, prompted this catastrophe? Why, after years of devotion and the cost involved in rearing a child, was the disclosure made at all?

Father pondered the attitude of Dinah's parents to find some explanation for their behaviour. He had always believed the theory that the real mother was the woman who brought up the child, not the one who bore it. It became clear that the adoptive parents resented the fact that their own daughters had been ignored by the suitor. Father refused to accept the doctrine that blood is thicker than water. It did not apply to this case, and he was sad and perplexed.

The logical procedure in this melodrama was to pacify Leibish's parents and induce them to accept Dinah as their daughter-in-law. They refused. Their rejection was based on the premise that Dinah had no name and no parents.

Father gave them several days to reconsider. Their answer remained an emphatic "no". They had all gathered in father's study when he rose to his full height and said, "Your objection is now based on the theory that your son's chosen bride has no name and no parents. Let me inform you that she now has both. My *rebbetzin* and I have meditated on this matter. We like Dinah enough to adopt her as our own daughter. Her name is Sarah, as was our Patriarch Abraham's wife."

And Sarah she became, with our surname entered on the *Ketubah*. Leibish's parents were satisfied and the marriage took place.

CHAPTER 7

Changes
in Our
Lives

OUR FAMILY WAS making strides in many walks of
life. Daniel did well as a ritual slaughterer. Sander
had graduated to a powerful rabbinical position and
was now studying law. Isaac was fast becoming a
very successful playwright and Israel was almost finished with his
rabbinical studies. All the girls were now married, except for me, and I
was busy assisting my father with his work. We had grown in many
ways since our arrival in Canada, and we often thought of our brother
Baruch, the only sibling to stay in Europe.

Father maintained contact with Baruch for a long time. Baruch
wrote regularly, and father supported his study at the university.
Sometimes father concealed money in photographs which he split
with a razor, resealed and sent to Europe. Then quite suddenly all
correspondence ceased.

My mother's hopes had rotated around Baruch for many years. The less news we had of him, the more she spoke about him, as if she were willing him to stay alive. Daily, she outlined plans for his future. He was to go to Palestine and help build a country. We were all aware that he might be dead and listening to mother's glowing hopes became an ordeal for us. Father used all his resources to trace Baruch. We knew that he had married and had a little daughter, Shoshana. At that time Uncle Reuben was still in Poland and acted as our major contact with my brother. Father wrote to Uncle Reuben asking him to employ professional help in his efforts to find Baruch.

We learned the horrible news. I happened to be staying in New York with Uncle Marvin when he received the letter from Europe. Uncle Reuben had not wanted to distress my parents, and so he had sent the tragic news to Uncle Marvin instead. Baruch and six other Jewish men had been shot as communists by the White Russians. Apparently, they had been ordered to strip, so that the Russians could ascertain that they were Jewish. Then they were murdered. We never found out where our loved one was buried, or whether he was buried at all!

Uncle Marvin told me these hideous facts and advised me to return home at once to break the shocking news to my parents. I was overcome with grief, but I was even more anxious about my mother's reaction than by the facts of my brother's death. I felt I couldn't tell father either because he would have to let mother know. When I returned home, I remained silent and suffered within myself. I became ill and unable to breathe. Father nursed me, propped me up in bed and held me.

My depression finally came to an end when Uncle Marvin regretted the task he had laid on my young shoulders and came to Montreal himself. He joined my father at my bedside. Father quietly and gently told me that he knew everything. A great burden was lifted from me.

Father decided to delay telling the awful news to mother. He learned that Baruch's wife Anna was alive and with her was their daughter Shoshana. Father hoped desperately that Baruch's child would act as solace to my mother. He contacted Anna and began to make plans for her and the child to come to us from Russia. With every effort we tried to keep the truth from mother, but she was suspicious and began watching us closely.

It was I who mailed father's correspondence. One day my mother stopped me on my way to mail a letter to Anna. I ran from the house. When I returned, the door to father's study was open. He and mother sat there stricken with grief. The tension was over. Mother never really recovered from Baruch's death, but she began to look to his child for consolation.

It took a long time for father to compile the necessary documents for Anna and the child's journey. Finally he finished, and the payment for the voyage was sent. My parents' anticipation was almost unbearable. Just as they had once made endless hopeful plans for Baruch, so they were constantly thinking of Anna and Shoshana. They prepared a room for them and made certain that their journey would be comfortable and happy. Nothing could be too good for Baruch's wife and child. In 1923 we received a cable informing us that they had left Warsaw and were on their way. Shoshana was nine years old.

My parents maintained an affectionate, solicitous and tolerant attitude towards Anna. They were not prepared for what took place. My parents were most concerned about making up to Anna and her child for the pain they had suffered at the loss of Baruch. He had written before his untimely death about their life together. He had lamented that Anna had had to live with him under conditions worse than those she had been accustomed to. He had written of Shoshana, to whom he had shown pictures of his parents and family so that she would recognize them when they were reunited. There was much love in Baruch!

The day finally came when we went to meet Anna and Shoshana at the station. How can I describe that day? Riva, mother and I had set out with flowers. Most of the passengers had gone, and we still had not yet spotted Anna and the child. At last we realized that the tall woman with an infant in her arms and a little girl beside her had to be Anna. She walked towards us with head bowed. Baruch had been dead for some years. If she had remarried, why hadn't we been told? We could not look at each other—the flowers dropped to the ground. We took the three newcomers home to face father.

Father never reproached Anna, nor did he immediately ask whose baby she had with her. It was a male child, and father insisted that he be circumcised. It surprised us to learn that Shoshana knew nothing at all about her father. We wanted her to know Baruch and the kind of man he was. We hoped that she could learn to revere his memory and keep it alive. My parents simply could not understand why the child had been kept in ignorance.

Anna declared that she was a communist. My parents were not upset—they were only concerned about Anna's reticence to explain her baby. Father broached the subject carefully, explaining that he was aware of the atrocities committed during the war, especially to women.

Anna announced that she had not, in fact, been raped at all. She had simply and willingly had a lover. When father relayed this reality to mother and me, his face took on a shrunken look, and he appeared to age many years in that one short moment.

It is perplexing trying to understand why Anna nurtured so much hostility towards my parents. They provided her with every comfort. She had known beforehand that they were orthodox Jews. Why had she come at all? Father had no objection to Anna's communist views. She had the right to any belief, as long as she treated the beliefs of others with deference and tolerance.

We all adored Shoshana. She ran about the house with her black hair flying, looking so like her father. Shoshana had forgotten all that her father had taught her. She was unable to speak a word of Yiddish which made communication very limited. She shared my room and bed, and I loved her dearly. My parents were very anxious that she learn more about her father and would in turn grow closer to us. Although she returned my affection, I could not seem to reach her.

While Anna reserved the right to think and act as she pleased, she did not extend this right to our family. Her behaviour became shocking, even vicious. Most unbearable were mealtimes. Anna was a chain smoker, and although she knew that it was forbidden on the Sabbath, she not only smoked incessantly, she obnoxiously blew smoke into father's face. She would air her thoughts on religion, saying that it was the root of all the evil in the world, and religious men like my father were monsters. She closed her opinionated comments by ridiculing my father's beard.

Father knew that Anna would have to leave our house. He tried desperately to make her understand how much Baruch's daughter meant to us. Anna's cry was, "Shoshana is my child." My father's answer was always, "I also have a right. She is all that is left of my son." He explained that the child was not to be taken away from her, that we would never invoke any prejudice against her mother to Shoshana. He simply wished that she be at least exposed to Judaism, so that at a mature age she would have a choice and the absolute right to make it. Anna put much effort into alienating her daughter from us, and my parents wanted so desperately to love and educate Shoshana.

Father explained that it was his duty to accept the role of father to Shoshana in light of his own son's death and to reserve the right to educate her in the religious beliefs of her departed parent. "A child is only entrusted to us for the duration of childhood," he said. "After that, it goes its own way."

It was all in vain. Anna left our house with the children, refusing any financial assistance. She made it quite clear that she would not permit Shoshana to visit us. This was a bitter blow, and the end of my parents' high hopes.

Before their departure, Father called Shoshana into his study. As a loving grandfather, he asked one favour of her, to recite the important Jewish prayer, the *Shema*: "Hear, O Israel, the Lord our God, the Lord is One." She laughed at him.

Years later mother received a phone call from the owner of a small shop where Shoshana worked after school. He knew of the family relationship and wanted to help reunite us. Mother rushed to the store and pleaded with Shoshana to visit us. She promised that we would make no demands, but Shoshana, crying, refused to utter a word. It was my parents' final attempt to reach her.

Shoshana was a clever girl and later became a communist agitator at her school. She was arrested many times for her convictions on the philosophy of brotherhood and humanism. My parents always remembered this child with the eternal hope that she would return. Often we would be sitting and chatting when the doorbell would ring at an unusual hour. My parents would look at one another with lingering hope and murmur, "Perhaps it is Shoshana." During their lifetime, she never returned.

It was the golden era of of the Yiddish theatre. Immigrants still did not speak the language of North American films, and even the children attended the Yiddish plays.

In those years, Yiddish as a language was the heart and soul of immigrant Jews. Most people still read only the Yiddish newspapers such as *The Jewish Daily Forward, The Day, The Morning Journal, The Amerikaner, The Tageblatt* and *The Freiheit*. Children conversed in Yiddish with their parents. They were still the first generation, and their thinking was tuned into that of their parents. The Yiddish language was alive; it throbbed in Jewish hearts.

In the Yiddish theatre the actors and the audience communicated on common ground. They cried, laughed, embraced, took sides and argued. Theatre was not only an escape, an outlet for the hardships of the time. It also provided a link with the past. Much as the immigrants were grateful for their precious freedom from persecution and pogroms, there lingered an attachment to traditions and the *alter heym* (old home). The Yiddish theatre reflected this and much more.

As theatre prospered, so did Isaac and Vera. By 1919 Isaac's plays were already famous and were performed in outstanding Yiddish theatres in Europe. That year Isaac moved his family to Winnipeg, to the Yiddish theatre there. In 1920 they went to Detroit and finally in 1921 to New York, the North American centre for Yiddish theatre. The most exciting times began; Isaac had arrived. His fame spread, not only as a writer, but as a lyricist. Isaac wrote plays and songs, and Vera performed. Often when an actor failed to appear, Isaac played the part himself. Both enjoyed much popularity during the ensuing years. Pictures of the two appeared on billboards, in restaurants, in newspapers and in Jewish homes. They were a husband and wife team who played and sang their way into the hearts of Jews in many American cities.

In 1932 after several years in New York, Isaac and Vera were at last able to open their own theatre. It was located in the heart of the Jewish district in the Lower East Side near Delancey Street. It was there that I met the great names in the Jewish theatrical world. What a wonderful experience!

Isaac worked with Sholom Secunda and Alexander Olshenetsky. He began to write exclusively for the finest artists of the times. The most gifted and renowned came to him, among them Lucy and Misha Garmon, Jenny Goldstein, Clara Young, Menashe Skulnik, Max Gable and Aron Lebedoff. Vera played with Moishe Oisher and Jacob Ben Ami.

The financial possibility of opening the Clinton Theatre was due to the fact that Isaac and Vera were successfully performing on radio for the "Saks Furniture Hour", which remained a popular program for fifteen years. Isaac supplied comedy with his beloved Yiddish characters. Vera became famous as "the *yiddishe shiksa*" (the Jewish-Gentile lady). Her voice and knowledge of Hebrew, Yiddish, Russian and Ukrainian songs brought her fame, as did her recordings.

It was Isaac who imbued me with a love for Yiddish theatre. Visiting him and Vera in New York was a special treat for me. Sometimes we walked arm in arm along the boardwalk at Coney Island. Usually we started out in the morning, when the din and confusion were still bearable. The benches were soon occupied, but many of the old people knew this and came prepared with folding chairs. They looked for the sun and greeted each other like long lost relatives. They did not waste time on the weather; they were agitators and politicians, and they talked about how the world should be run. Sometimes they were so emphatic that their chairs collapsed. Isaac always enjoyed speaking with the old. "Just listen to the wisdom. They are the most interesting of all, for they represent history."

Best of all, I loved the East Side. Those memories come alive for me. I see us on Delancey Street, Clinton Street, Hester and Orchard. We stop at pushcarts. Isaac points to elderly Jews with black velvet skull caps, their *tzitzis* blowing in the wind. It is hot, their faces perspire; they are completely oblivious of discomfort. When they quote prices for their wares, it is in the singsong tone of the Talmud.

Walking in the streets, I am excited by all I see. There are barrels of sour pickels and herring, which one can buy by the piece. Pedestrians promenade, relishing with zest, not only the food, but each other. Women sit on front steps nursing their babies, and no one takes notice. Black-haired black-eyed girls walk by, arm in arm, casting shy, furtive glances at the young men who pass. Those accompanied by men, indicate that they are either engaged or married. I marvel at the expressions on their faces — there is much joy and laughter.

The Jews behind the pushcarts disappear in the afternoons, still pursuing their Talmudic studies, as they had in the old country. The wives then take over the work, thinking nothing wrong with such a procedure. After all, they have grown up with the understanding that the husband is the head of the house, and the more learned he is, the more prestigious the family.

Something took place inside me whenever I visited New York. I felt a deep identification with the people I encountered on the East Side. They wore their Jewishness with a pride and joy that affected me deeply and made me feel that I belonged.

I am reluctant to say farewell to this period of my life. I see father feeding the birds in winter. They would gather on the window sill and father would draw me towards him, place an arm around me and say, "Do you hear the birds chirping, and do you know what they are saying? It is Leah, Leah."

One of the chores I loved was to wash father's hair, his beard and his *payess* (side earlocks). I massaged his scalp until he begged for mercy. Then I would dry his beard. It was a gentle beard, like father. When I finished, I would divide his beard into sections, and we would figure out which child occupied which section. I would say, "Father, pray for a miracle — that your beard grows larger to make room now for your grandchildren. They, too, will need a spot on your beard."

I desperately want to recapture the years with my parents and with my young children. The future is ever a mystery. I did not know that when I married I would leave behind me the happiest part of my life. I would never again feel the serenity, the same belief in the future. I would be harrassed, I would experience despair, frustration, regret, agony, heartache and terrible unhappiness.

# PART FOUR

CHAPTER 8

♅ —— *Marriage*
*and*
*Children*

TIME DID NOT STAND STILL. I was growing into womanhood. My parents began to think of marriage for
me. Father was determined to find what he
described as "a special kind of man" for me.

I believe implicitly that my father thought only of my happiness and
welfare when he followed his own dictates with Ezra, the young man
who was Israel's tutor in the Hebrew language. I could have climbed
high mountains with Ezra. I think of him with a longing that has never
subsided. A sensitive face, with deep-set, penetrating eyes, of medium
height, slender, quiet, with a penetrating mind that was a delight to
explore. He was a student of law with a promising future but at the
time he came to our home, he was very poor. It would have taken
some years before he would have been able to give me the supposed
good things of life. Too bad my father had misunderstood what actually
constituted the good things of life.

We would have managed. But father would not have me struggle. I was seventeen years old, and I had to wait. The young teacher was sent away. How can a seventeen year old, granted a sensitive even intelligent girl, overrule a man like my father — brilliant, understanding and fully schooled in the way of life? How could I question his opinion?

It is said that when a clever man makes a mistake, it turns out to be a bad one. And bad, it was. If I had only been granted a few years of a loving and compatible union. How that would have changed my life! Unfortunately father overlooked the admonition, "An ignorant man should not marry the daughter of a priest" (Code of Jewish Law).

Among the staunch supporters of my father was the family Willensky. There were five brothers who shared a business. The firm was engaged in the sale of lumber and building materials. The three eldest brothers, Pinchus, Mechel and Asher, were irrevocably joined to my parents and myself. They played an important part in the orthodox Jewish community and possessed qualities which made them outstanding, not only as members of the community, but as family men as well. I married into that family.

At the time we arrived in Montreal, these three families had reached the peak of their prosperity. They were financially sound and contributed generously to synagogues, Hebrew schools and charitable organizations. As a result, they were regarded with respect and held in esteem.

While the three brothers were alike in their religious beliefs, in other ways they were totally different. The eldest brother Pinchus was aggressive and astute. He headed the firm. Mechel was a quiet man. Asher, the one who travelled for the business, was seldom in Montreal. These three brothers were very close.

The lives of our family and theirs were entirely dissimilar. Between my parents, there existed a strong bond. My father consulted my mother and shared his life outside the home sphere with her. There was a zest and excitement in my father's profession that was part of our everyday lives.

Though the Willensky family ties were as strong as ours, there was a vast difference between us on the role of a wife. Their wives bore the children, catered to their men and kept the house. Their world revolved only around their husbands and children. Babies were born every year. There was little or no outside help. Household chores required so much energy and were so time-consuming they left little leisure time for external matters. The wives felt no resentment, since their mode of life was similar to that of other families with whom they came in contact.

In Pinchus Willensky's household it was the father who wielded the power. He alone resolved the future of his children. He could be understanding and lovable, or stern, cruel and unyielding. This placed the children at the mercy of a despot. It all hinged on the nature and character of the man, for he was the head of the family. He regarded his children as his personal property. This headstrong man ruled his children with an iron hand. No one dared to defy him.

But Pinchus Willensky also had much to recommend him. He had educated himself to a degree where he was aware of events in everyday existence, with Jewish communal life his prime interest. He was a dogmatic, religious man. While not versed in *Talmud*, he diligently studied the Five Books of Moses. He refused to read or tolerate a commentary or criticism on anything relating to the Torah. Any reference to great thinkers meant a diverse opinion, which resulted in an argument.

What impressed me most in the years that I knew Pinchus Willensky was his unwavering confidence in the after world. That belief never weakened. So secure was he in that conviction, that he had absolutely no fear of death. It was as though he almost looked forward to dying, so eloquently did he speak of the true world. So devout was he that his greatest joy was to conduct synagogue services. He performed that duty with love and devotion to God.

But what happens when a man of high principles is confronted with conflicting and hopeless circumstances? Do all his lofty ideals and his impregnable faith vanish? Do all the commandments he preached evaporate into thin air? It is so easy to be good when life goes well. When we are faced with a real dilemma and are obliged to make the choice of either right or wrong, can we differentiate between the two?

Father had developed a stronq friendship with Mechel Willensky. It was he who paved the way for the match between Aron, Pinchus' son, and myself. Retracing the passage of time, I can now think dispassionately. I realize that I, as a person, did not play an important part. To the Willensky family, I represented *yiches*. Even today, established families strive to enter the domain of Talmudic lineage. It is a "connection". *Yiches* still takes precedence over money, real estate or stocks.

My parents wanted a life of ease for me. Unfortunately, they failed to look beyond that. It was a delusion. There is no doubt in my mind that if the Willensky family had not been so affluent, my misguided and tragic marriage would never have taken place. The fact remains that, while *yiches* was the goal of the Willenskys, money, with the best of intentions, was the dominant factor on my side. It was a reversal of standards!

My husband Aron and I were introduced when I was barely seven-teen, and he was close to twenty. He was a short, slender young man with a somewhat dark complexion, brown eyes, sharp features, a wide mouth and thick lips. He was the eldest of twelve children and employed as a bookkeeper in the Willensky firm.

Aron did not talk much, so I rarely knew what he was thinking. He had a sister my age who was always with us, which made any effort at communication impossible. I admit that Aron and I never had a serious conversation before we were married. Later he was as unhappy with me as I was with him. I hope he forgave me for having married him. It never should have been. I was the dominant party, and he was the recessive. The onus of guilt still rests on me!

Was I such a bargain? It depends on your viewpoint. Neither a pretty girl, nor was I homely. Two big eyes, soft and pleading, yet with the stern look of a school teacher, a nose too large for my face, a lovely skin which I still have, straight brown hair, a slender neck with a head held high, short but not stocky—I always moved quickly and still do. A little wit, a little charm, always anxious to talk, I had an unquenchable thirst for knowledge.

My father-in-law took me to a jeweller where he purchased a diamond ring and pendant for me. He furnished a flat for us including all the household utensils. The cost of the wedding was also paid for by Aron's father. It was a beautiful wedding; generosity flourished. If bad times had not pressured him, it is unlikely that I would have seen the negative side of Pinchus Willensky.

Before my betrothal, business discussions had taken place between Aron's father, his brother Mechel and father. The result was a verbal agreement made by Pinchus that his son Aron would be given a share in the business after the wedding. Aron was to become a partner. This announcement was sanctioned with a handshake—a gentlemen's agreement. Here was my father, a man who sat in on countless *Din Torahs* where business associates sued each other with various claims. Notwithstanding, my clever, experienced father took the word of Aron's father that his son was to share in his business without a written agreement.

Despite the preparations for the wedding, I decided to speak to my parents about Aron. I was convinced that I was about to contract a lifetime union with a young man who was not suitable for me. I told my parents, "I am afraid of this marriage. The more I see of Aron the more doubts I have. What worries me most is that he seems such a boy, so young. We also have so little in common." Father reassured me, "He comes from a good family. He will provide adequately for you, and you will teach him to like what you like." My mother approved vehemently, "The Willensky family is well-to-do. Look how generous they are and see all the gifts they have showered on you." In fact, my marriage was the first one in our family with which my parents were pleased. Still I felt uncertain, but I had implicit faith in my parents. I was not forced into the marriage, but I was persuaded. My parents hoped Aron would grow on me.

Aside from the wedding guests, the festivities and the ceremony, the most dramatic part I lovingly recall was the waltz I danced with my father. The memory lingers on. Father was a graceful man, and we danced in perfect harmony. The guests stood on chairs and tables, all keen to catch a glimpse of father dancing with the bride. The wedding was a spectacle. The year was 1924.

I think back and wonder how I could have been so dull witted, so ignorant of sex! I was fairly intelligent; I had read extensively. Yet faced with the actual sex act, I was not only reluctant, I was terrified!

Prior to my wedding my mother explained the rules pertaining to the observation of the period after menstruation which led to the immersion known as the *mikva* bath. "It is written unto a woman in her menstrual uncleanliness, thou shalt not come near her" (Leviticus XVIII 19). She is considered menstrually unclean until she counts the seven clean days and takes the proper bath of immersion (Code of Jewish Law). I found even a discussion about sex both embarassing and intrusive. Possibly I had this feeling because my mother had neither discussed nor alluded to sex before, though I was her constant companion and very close to her.

Before the wedding, Chia came to my rescue. She told me I was too fastidious and initiated me into the rudiments of the sex act. She undressed me and did her utmost to clarify what intercourse entailed and very simply explained how it was done. So much for my education!

There had long existed a dubious custom among very observant Jews that a male member of the groom's family, usually the father, found it incumbent upon himself to visit the bridal couple the day after the wedding to ascertain whether the bride was a virgin. This was done by checking the bed sheet for blood stains.

Sure enough, Aron's father and uncle came strutting in, their faces intent as if to perform some religious rite. However, those poor men had no idea that they were dealing with an unusual bride. They were

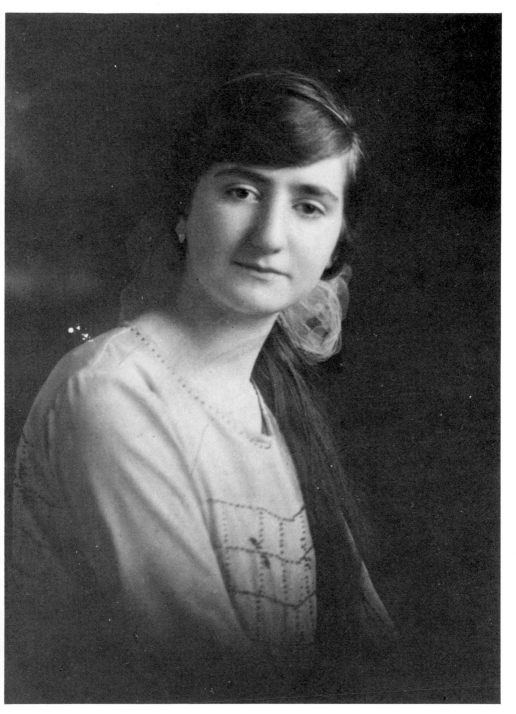

*Leah. Circa 1920.*

*Left to right: my mother, Chia, Isaac, Baruch, and the son who died. Circa 1900.*

*My father and mother before our departure to Canada. Circa 1912.*

*Left to right: Leah, Riva, Vera, Chia, Israel, my mother, and Elie. Circa 1914.*

*My mother, Sarah Gitel Rosenberg. Circa 1914.*

*My father, Rabbi Jehudah Yudel Rosenberg. Circa 1914.*

*Circa 1940.*

# The Canadian
# Jewish Chronicle

## THE NATIONAL JEWISH WEEKLY

*The first and foremost Anglo-Jewish Weekly in Canada :: Successor to the Canadian Jewish Times, Founded 1897*

Montreal, Friday February 13, 1931        Volume XVIII, Number 39

Seventieth Anniversary of Rabbi Jehudah
Rosenberg, Local Talmudist and Scholar

Circulating in Montreal, Toronto, Winnipeg, Ottawa, Halifax, Vancouver and other Canadian Cities

*Anna. Circa 1912.*

*My brother, Baruch,
in university uniform.
Circa 1915.*

*The good friends, Chia (left) and Vera*
*Circa 1915.*

*Vera and Isaac. Circa 1912.*

*Vera and Isaac. Circa 1930.*

BOTTOM ROW, *left to right: Leah, Chia, Riva, mother, father, Israel, Elie, Daniel's wife, Daniel.*
MIDDLE ROW: *Aron, Ari, a cousin, a nephew, Mendel, Hannah, Mark.*

*Three generations. Circa 1928.*

*Circa 1937.*

*My sons. Circa 1933.*

*Circa 1933.*

*Isaac and my mother during her illness. Circa 1940.*

*Circa 1942.*

*St. Agathe. Circa 1946.*

*My brother, the rabbi, at the Passover Seder table. Circa 1975.*

mystified by the fact that there was no sign of blood on the bed sheet. It never occurred to them that I would have changed the sheets, if only to thwart them. I was so angry at their intrusion of my privacy. They left completely mystified, their holy mission uncompleted.

I knew before my marriage that we were terribly mismatched. All the reasons for the failure of our marriage stemmed from the stark differences in our characters. I was strong and spirited, and Aron was weak and passive. I could not abide weakness. Even as a child I wanted to walk with my face against the wind and to conquer it. I longed to marry a man with whom I could climb high mountains. I was a fighter. It was not that I wanted to prove my strength, rather I wanted to use it. As a wife I was eager to give of myself so that my husband could achieve his goals faster through my assistance. In the end my strength would prove my weakness. I vented my heartaches, my frustrations and disillusion on Aron relentlessly.

Ever present was my father's place in my life. During my marriage while my parents were still alive, and especially during my pregnancies, it was my father who supplied the love my husband never gave me. He did not rob Aron of his rights; Aron never exercised them. My father tried to succour my spirit, my hunger for love, my search for sensitivity, my desire to explore and my hunger to communicate. True, I fashioned the role of a husband in my father's image, but Aron was so far from being my father's equal. If I had married a man who was a scholar, he and father would have formed a relationship of which I would have been a part. Like my mother I had cherished the hope of marriage to a Talmudist. I wanted to give of myself. For me that precious role was denied.

It is also a fact that my parents' married life was instrumental in influencing my own perception of marriage. It was like a vision I saw when I looked into the mirror of my life. Theirs was a mating in which there was hardly a single flaw. Perhaps it was not a fair basis of comparison. My parents were exceptional people, so theirs was an exceptional marriage. It must have affected the unhappy married lives of my sisters as well. We were witnesses to the love, joy and compatibility they shared, and somehow our own lives were sadly lacking. It is a mystery how the good in life can have a bad effect on us.

For my mother, marriage was the only goal of a woman. My father was the base of her life. Even now I wonder how she would have reacted to a husband she found wanting. My mother was extremely aggressive. Despite all her avowals that one must accept fate, I doubt if she would have been submissive. The estimation in which she held father never lessened her role, for mother played a very definite part in father's career. Both cherished a deep appreciation of the other's qualities and contributions to their individual successes.

If I examine my mother, in all honesty I cannot say that I disagree with her role as a wife. But then I am prejudiced for it involves my father. I could only visualize my own conduct and identify with my mother if I had been married to a man of my father's calibre. Still I do not believe I would ever have wanted a career based solely on being a wife and mother. Early in life I began to maintain an identity as an individual, a person. I wanted to proclaim that I was responsible for myself.

There was no bond, no closeness between Aron and me — we lived together. There was acute suffering caused by the lack of emotion on both sides, I am certain. Aron felt the absence of sexual responsiveness on my part. What I could not clarify to myself was how I could go through the act without love or understanding. That act did nothing for me. I was able to passively separate myself from it. Yet I never ceased to ponder how that could be. I was fully aware that sex was not a passive act; I longed for passion and satisfaction and wondered if I would ever experience it. In my subconscious was the constant hope that I would free myself from Aron. I looked forward to release. I also speculated if, when that time arrived, I would still be sexually motivated. I wanted to experience those feelings. I knew Aron felt keenly the non-fulfilment. He was sexually vibrant.

If a marriage is devoid of love, there is despair. When added to that, there is the absence of a livelihood, it becomes a catastrophe. Fear can destroy one's soul! The necessities of life — rent payments, food purchases, doctor's fees and medication for sick children — I lived it all in sheer terror.

The first years of my married life were free from monetary worries. But the Depression began for me earlier than 1929. The lucrative business of the Willensky family suffered a painful setback. They never recovered. It seemed they had invested a considerable amount of money in rubber which they hoped to sell to a foreign country at a substantial profit. This profit was never realized. The venture failed; the investment swallowed all their resources. The rubber stock became worthless, and the effort and struggle to carry on the business began. The seven lean years had swallowed the seven fat years.

My father broached the subject of Aron's share in the business. Aron's father denied that he had ever even made reference to such a promise. No partnership existed at any time. What was of primary importance was that, as a result of the promised partnership, Aron had never been trained in any other capacity to earn a living. In all fairness, how could he cope with a family? Aron did not lack ability. Unfortunately he was bereft of initiative, and this rendered him incapable.

After our marriage Aron became a truck driver for his father's firm. It soon became apparent that the father regarded his son as a burden. Aron became an employee with a salary which did not always materialize — it was paid in dribblets. I could never rely on money for rent, food or coal to heat the flat. Collectors appeared at our door who threatened to shut off the water and discontinue supplying gas. I became desperate.

My parents began to supply us with weekly food parcels. The realization that they had to assist us overwhelmed me with grief. My father was no longer a young man. The idea of accepting anything I did not earn or that did not come through the labour of my husband, who was duty-bound to care for me, made me ill. Now began the agony that was to last for many years. A void of darkness settled over me — an enveloping bitterness that engulfed me like a swamp. What I found most painful of all was that I was forced to accept assistance from my parents. Charity! I wanted to die!

Father and mother suffered with me. They could not separate themselves from me. We were joined in a bond both physical and psychological. I began to blame them for my unsuccessful marriage. I embittered their lives. This memory leaves me sad. It slowly came to my parents that they were responsible for my marriage. All had been done in love and good faith, but it had been a blunder of the first magnitude. They had married me into a rich family, but had never looked at the person to whom they were marrying me. I let loose a torrent of reproach. It accomplished nothing. It made my parents unhappy and filled me with remorse.

In order to save his business and hold on to the property that housed it, Pinchus needed money, and his methods of obtaining it were ingenious. He had numerous systems for raising money. One of these was cheque changing. He would give Aron a cheque for a sizable amount, out of which was to come his salary. It was my duty to go to the little corner grocery to do some shopping and cash the cheque.

The owner of the shop was a young, overworked woman whose husband suffered from a heart ailment. She was the breadwinner. She cashed the cheques, but they were returned by the bank. Aron's father instructed me to tell the shopkeeper to continue redepositing the cheques. It took weeks before they were made good. Pinchus used the money that was not his to use. Finally, the shopkeeper regretfully told me that she could not cash any more cheques. The inevitable arguments ensued, but I needed food. Eventually, I refused to take more cheques. I could not accept everything from my parents. So, I had to find another grocery shop.

How I hated it all! The life, the cheques, the continuous quarrelling which culminated with the same old phrase, "If you don't like it, go back to your parents." I stopped counting the times I returned home during my married life.

When father gave Aron money, my father-in-law helped himself to it. I lost all respect for my husband. This was not due to his inability to provide for us. It was the weakness in his character and his dependence on his father that I hated.

And what did I want from him? He could give me only what he was capable of giving. It is like growing to a certain height. Nature allows one to grow so tall, and no taller, to go so far and no farther. What gave me the right to demand of him what was not in his power to give?

For me, matters progressed from bad to worse. I lived in loneliness as far as my marriage was concerned. Outwardly, I went about my life in what seemed a normal fashion. Yet I was divided into parts, each one a separate existence. One I shared with my parents, another was the life I lived within myself. The third was my life with my children.

I had two children. When I carried my first child, my Ari, I was overwhelmed with the miracle of a life within a life. The first time I felt life within me, I stood transfixed in wonder. There were small ripples on my stomach, which I stood watching. Then I grew, that is my stomach grew and expanded, and I began to fear that I was about to be devoured by my own body. I stood in front of a mirror and congratulated myself as if I was the only woman to become a mother.

How I loved the thought of motherhood, someone of my own to love, fondle, caress and talk to. I counted the months and waited with excitement, as did my parents. The last few days before my due date I spent in my parents' home. They hovered over me as if the messiah were about to appear.

Then began a comedy of errors. My parents had to attend a banquet where father was to speak. They did not want to stay there for long, so we arranged a "set-up".

Mother outlined the details. "Now, Leah, here is the telephone number. Call at eight o'clock. By that time the dinner will be over and father will have spoken. You will ask to give me a message that you are on your way to the hospital and that we must come home. That will give us an excuse to leave."

Off they went and an hour later my labour pains actually did begin. Aron became nervous and shouted, "Come to the hospital right away." But no, I had to call my parents. Yet how could I make the message clear that I was *really* in labour and for them to hurry home. I could not. The message was conveyed to them as arranged. They waited an hour and came home.

In the meantime the pains kept coming and Aron took me to the hospital. Finally my baby arrived! A child had emerged from my body! It was flesh of my flesh, mind of my mind and heart of my heart. I looked at my son, a little whisp of flesh with two big eyes and a beautiful face.

At the time that I became pregnant with my second child, I experienced a great deal of guilt. What right did I have to bring another child into the world? No child asks to be born. Each child deserves the right to a good life. With a mother full of doubts, a father lacking a sense of responsibility, what chance did my children have?

More than the subjugation and submission that enveloped me, I resented desperately that my unhappiness reflected on my children. I was short with them. I was unable to enjoy them. I was hampered by constant fear—the uncertainty of what the next day would bring. If I was ever offered a choice of which part of my life I would choose to relive, it would be this period of time. I would wish for a freedom from care that would enable me to enjoy my children when they were small and dependent on my love and understanding.

Mother warned me not to tell father of my second pregnancy. I had been cautioned by my parents to avoid having another child. We had begun to consider divorce seriously. They were right but it was as if I were driven.

It was mostly due to my deprivation of love—I craved a nearness, for I was consumed with an urge to touch and be tender. I wanted to give of myself and, hopefully, receive in return. The need to love surged up in me like the waves of a mighty ocean. I felt I had failed in my marriage. Having children would give me a second chance.

My worried, tense state caused my mother much concern, and she sought to console me. "Leah, do not look so sad. When a child is born, he brings with him his own destiny, his own ability and his own luck."

I think of the love and tenderness father lavished on me during the depressed condition I was enduring. When I was pregnant, he told me how beautiful I was. Actually I was as big as a house. All through the nine long months, he would place his hand on my stomach to feel the baby move. As the delivery of my first child drew near, father said he had had a dream. One of his old teachers informed father that I would have a boy and asked that the child be named after him. And so my first son became Ari. With the second child, another of his teachers came to him in a dream, said I would bear a son again and asked that the child be named after him. And so my second son became Moshe.

All through my second pregnancy, I kept wondering how to meet the expense of the birth. The fee of the obstetrician at that time was fifty dollars. I was afraid to be admitted as a public patient, as I had suffered a dangerous miscarriage in the time between the births of the two children. I had my baby and somehow, the bills were met.

As with my older son, father circumcised the child. Although he had a slight muscle tremour, his hands were still steady for circumcision. I could not bear to have someone else as a *mohel*. It would have hurt both father and me.

While they were still very young, I set about telling my children Jewish stories. When I lacked money for children's books, I used my imagination. I described our festivals and taught them prayers. They were raised in the strict orthodox fashion but never with fear — always with love and sense of beauty. My efforts were towards their Hebrew studies. My hopes ran high that they would enter the rabbinate. It was a dream from which I awakened very early. Nevertheless, heritage roots had been deeply planted. Nothing could ever erase that.

In truth I kept my children in what amounted to a Jewish isolation. I imbued them with a strong feeling for our faith, regaled them with Jewish stories, concentrated on prayers and blessings. They wore the *tallis kuten* (small prayer shawls) in which they slept. Their skull caps were always on their heads. At three years, they recited the four questions in perfect Hebrew at the Passover table.

I did not take motherhood lightly. I was very close to my children and kept watch on their education. However, I was harassed financially which made me insecure and unhappy. It became an overpowering desire to see that my children's future would be assured — that they would never suffer deprivation.

I vowed to myself that I would move mountains to help prepare them to take their place in life, to seek fulfilment in suitable careers. Regardless of the scarcity of funds, I sent my sons to Hebrew schools where there were capable teachers. I went without, always to promote and encourage the education of my sons. Perhaps I did it as much for

25 Rutherford Road South, Unit #1, Brampton, Ontario L6W 3J3
Phone: 905-450-9033 • Fax: 905-450-0754 • email: camelot@interlog.com

myself as for them. I wanted them to excel; I must have overpowered them. I was ambitious for them, but in all fairness to myself, I did not think of ambition in terms of large sums of money or harm to others. I did not want them to struggle — just as my parents had never wanted me to struggle.

Despite all the complexities I encountered, my children were the joy of my life. My little boys were a delight, clever with large eyes. I did not have to urge them to study or read; they early displayed an innate intelligence. They were gentle children.

Aron came to life with our children. He was a good and loving father, a companion and friend to his sons. He spoke kindly to them though he could never communicate with me. The children filled a place in their father's life which I was never able to penetrate.

Every Saturday they went with their father to synagogue services. They knew and understood all the festivals. They particularly loved the holiday of Simchat Torah that celebrates the conclusion of the year's reading of the Law. The children waved their flags and watched as their elders marched with the precious Torah Scroll.

And there was the presence of my father. He loved the boys. They would sit on his lap while he drew pictures for them. Each one received what mother called a *yidele* (a little Jew with a long beard), drawn by my father. Father would lift his beard to pass over the little faces of my children, a gesture they loved.

Summers we spent in the Laurentian Mountains. There we occupied a rented cottage in Shawbridge or Piedmont. Those summers are still unforgettable. My children and I were in daily contact with my parents. In the evenings we went for walks. Father held each child by the hand, explaining the Godliness of nature. Always he turned to them, "*Yingelech* (little boys), let us make a blessing, for God created all this beauty around us."

Some afternoons we would all sit on the grass, and father would read poetry. The children nestled near him. Most of all father talked about the beauty and the mysticism of the True World. "Do you know," he began, "when souls have found their abode in the True World, most of all they sit and study Torah. It often happens that departed parents are interrupted and called from their perusal of the Prophets. A voice says, "Ezekiel and Dvosha, your children have arrived with a *bakoshe* (request). And then," father continued, "the parents reluctantly rise and enter their graves and listen." My children would gaze up at father with so much love, their eyes filled with emotion and wonder that this extraordinary man was their *zaide* (grandfather).

During my father's lifetime Ari was already of an age where he was able to derive a strong feeling for his *zaide* which has remained with him. There was five years difference between my children so that my older son received more attention and recalls better the likeness of my father. I think with harsh regret that Moshe missed a deeper sense of the greatness of my father. To him, my father is an elusive memory. I often deplore the fact that my younger son was not yet of an age to develop a closeness to my father. In view of the career he chose, his inspiration and gift as a writer would have benefited considerably from a closer relationship with this extraordinary man.

I always knew the boys were gifted; they had an innate cleverness. They were avid readers, so books circulated in the house, and my education received stimulation from theirs. In appearance Ari was a mixture of his father and myself. Moshe had many of his father's features, but resembled me closely. Both were extremely serious and affected by world conditions. This was offset by a delightful, penetrating sense of humour.

From early childhood my children learned to think, to analyse, and to make their own decisions. We delighted in their cleverness. When I was pregnant with Moshe, Ari knew there was a baby on the way. It was the Festival of Succot, the holiday when we bless the *esrog* (citron) and *lulav* (palm branch). It is the custom for a pregnant woman to bite off the *pitem* (protruding top of the *esrog*) to promote an easy childbirth. So father brought the *esrog* for me to bite the *pitem*. Ari looked on and said in a thoughtful manner, "*Zaide*, I know we are Jewish, but what happens to pregnant women who are not Jewish? How can they have an easy childbirth?" Father was pleased. "Very good, Ari. Non-Jewish women have the same rights as Jewish women. All they have to do to ensure an easy childbirth is to bite off the *pitem* of an *esrog*."

Moshe was an early protestor. One Sabbath he decided to visit his paternal grandparents. Since that was a distance away, it meant going by streetcar. We did not ride on streetcars on the Sabbath. Moshe would not accept a no. So he turned to my father. "*Zaide*, the streetcar does not run only for us. Many passengers get on the car, so we do not hire it. Why then can we not get on the streetcar on the Sabbath, since it does not take us alone?" Father looked at the little fellow; he was so very young. "A Talmud head! He will bear watching."

I remember an amusing incident that occurred when Moshe was at Talmud Torah school. The principal, a very able, cultured man, looked despairingly at me. "You know I can easier cope with a hundred students than with Moshe. Never can I get the better of him or win an argument." What now? I thought. "Here is a boy injured by another boy who threw a snowball packed with some heavy ingredient. He must be punished. Moshe is the only boy who saw it happen, and he refused to tell me who the culprit was. Can you ask him to do so?"

"No, Moshe has to decide for himself. He is usually right." And I made my way out the door.

The boys were devoted to me, and I loved them with an overpowering love. I was an intense person, so pent up emotions flowed from me. Because my marriage was unhappy, I was in constant fear that I would smother my sons with love, or I would add to the love I naturally bore them, the love that should have been directed toward their father.

My sons turned out very well. Not due to my efforts, perhaps despite them. I cannot take the credit for what my children have accomplished today; they, themselves, are responsible. They had the desire, the thirst for knowledge and the capabilities. I was merely the vehicle who brought them forth. Heredity is a riddle which I cannot solve. Perhaps my children can explain it better than I.

# CHAPTER 9

## *Depression*

I LOOK AGAIN into the mirror of my past. It is the early 1930s, not long before the demon Hitler came to power. I see my parents seated before the radio, listening to Hitler. Israel and I cast frightened glances at each other. Not so father. He murmurs over and over again, "The world is not mad. The world will not allow such a beast to come to power." Thank God, he did not live to witness the Holocaust.

The Depression began. It ate itself into the very being of the people. It seemed to me that I was isolated in my suffering, but everybody must have experienced the same feelings. It was a period of intense agony for millions.

Our mode of living bore no resemblance to either comfort or luxury. All worked hard just to live. Hunger, deprivation, shame and anxiety reigned. There were no jobs available and consequently no security. People lost their savings, their homes and the small businesses that they had struggled for years to attain. What became most heart-rending were the looks of despair one encountered on familiar faces.

Perhaps the kind of people we were accounted for our survival. We still had the taste of the old country, where living conditions were an ordeal to be faced with fortitude, hope, stoicism and courage.

There is a Yiddish proverb, "A poor person is likened unto a corpse". I cannot think of a more adequate description. To be poor is to be powerless. Poverty is demeaning, demoralizing. It saps the strength and destroys the will to live. It makes one a beggar and deprives one of the joy of life. The development of an artist does not flourish while he or she starves in an attic. Poverty does not bring forth the genius. This is a misconception. Another fallacy is that one's character develops when in need. Often it deteriorates.

Poverty affected me deeply. I am still a hoarder. My cupboards are packed with cans of food "just in case". Fear is so ingrained in me that I seldom finish a meal without leaving part of it, "just in case".

It became necessary for my family to move from house to house. How was I to pay the rent? The moving was done at night to avoid detection. I searched for housing on side streets where the rent would be lower. I worked endlessly to make each place a home, painting and cleaning while the tears ran down my face.

My unhappiness reflected on the children. I was often not a fit mother being nervous, impatient and sad. I was abrupt with them. I was unable to enjoy them, for I was beset by fear of what the next day would bring.

I sometimes feel that I am on trial with myself. If I had concentrated my efforts on earning a livelihood instead of depending on my husband, how much heartache I would have spared myself. But I had no vocational training and had been raised in an atmosphere where the husband provides for his family.

Father was able to find odd jobs for Aron from time to time. Sadly, Aron made no effort on his own behalf. He was not lazy; he feared failure. Perhaps that is why he clung so desperately to his father.

Father and I had constant discussions about Aron's dependency on his father, a man for whom my father had developed an overwhelming dislike. "You must understand, Leah, that Aron's father directed the lives of his children. He did their thinking, thereby weakening their ability to face responsibility. So we must now take Aron away from his father's influence and lock the door."

There was only one hope for me. Aron had to leave his father, to sever all business relations with him. I thought that if he could change in that way, other changes would follow, and we could make a go of our marriage. So I pulled tenaciously in that direction. I was, and am, not one to give up easily. I tried peacefully, quietly; that failed. I threatened to leave; that made no impact. But never will I say that I did not try. I raged, I fought, I tore myself apart. I thought we could learn to work together. I waged a desperate fight to preserve our marriage.

Aron was very good at figures, and I was convinced that he could master accountancy. In those days higher education was not compulsory, and I was confident that he could succeed. My parents agreed to assist us. I made every effort to instill confidence in Aron. I failed miserably.

Father gave money to Aron on many occasions so that Aron could go into business himself. This did not help either. The money always fell into the hands of Aron's father. I tried to make father understand that he was contributing to Aron's weakness and his dependency on his father. The result was that father often hid the true facts from me.

On one occasion Pinchus came to father to discuss a new business idea for Aron. He was to manufacture bricks for the construction of houses. The amount needed for investment was 1000 dollars. The manufacture of the bricks was to be done in the back yard of Pinchus' house. That meant no rent — it sounded good to father.

At that time 1000 dollars was a considerable amount of money. I pointed out that Aron knew nothing about bricks, and that the money would simply go to his father. Father insisted on handing over a cheque to Aron for 1000 dollars, admonishing him to take good care of the money. It was to be considered a loan.

The following day, the money was already in the hands of Aron's father. This time my father demanded an explanation. The two worthy brothers, Pinchus and Mechel, both appeared and their explanation was thus. Aron had entrusted the cheque to his father who was to cash it for him. Immediately thereafter, the two brothers were held up, and the cheque was stolen from them. They expected my father to believe them. It was incredible. Their treatment of Aron and their various manipulations were not only base, they were immoral.

Later, when I confronted Aron with the abominable lie his father and uncle had told, he defended his father. To manufacture bricks was too difficult a way to earn a living. His father would soon think of an easier method.

This was not yet the end. Riva was continually on the lookout for a profitable business deal. My father-in-law knew she had money, and so a deal was concocted. He managed to convince her that the money would be invested in merchandise so desirable that its price would soar. They would make a small fortune. She was to be the silent partner; Aron was to be the working one.

Riva was very financially shrewd, which proves what a smooth talker Aron's father was. If he could persuade Riva, he could accomplish anything. She handed the money over to Aron. The merchandise was never purchased. The money passed from Aron to his father.

What my parents and I experienced as a result! I can still see the scenes which took place. It was as if a volcano had errupted as Riva gave vent to her shock, dismay and bitter disappointment. She paced the floor and threatened revenge. She wanted Pinchus arrested. Once again my father came to the rescue paying Riva the money Aron owed her.

Dire consequences followed this episode. I became so nervous that my parents were alarmed. I let loose a tirade against my father and mother for the agony of my marriage. At least one problem was solved. This last incident marked the end of the money giving by my father and the phony business deals.

Selma's husband, Yossel, was doing well in Hamilton, and father wrote to him asking if he would either employ Aron or find a job for him in Hamilton. That was a painful step for my parents to even consider. It would mean that eventually my children and I would have to leave Montreal to join Aron. A feeling of sadness pervaded the home of my parents, but father realized that such a drastic measure had to be taken. My life, as it was, had become unbearable.

All the worry was needless. Aron did not leave Montreal. He was saved by his father who promised once again that he would give Aron a job and a weekly salary. If Aron left for Hamilton, he said with a pious expression, his son would become a *goy*, and then he would have to disown him.

Through all the crisis, Aron sat quietly by, as though these events did not concern him at all. To my amazement Aron told me that it was all my fault that he could not make a living. His father had informed him that a livelihood is a wife's luck, so if I had no luck I must suffer the consequences. I knew the battle was lost.

I first began to think of divorce when I felt the erosion of my respect for Aron. But at the time I felt it was an unattainable dream. Where would I go with two young children? I could not become a complete burden to my parents.

My father regarded divorce as a possibility. My mother was vehemently opposed. A continuous dispute developed between us. Mother could not bear to see me so unhappy. To her it was all due to my stubborness and the wrong conception of religion, marriage and God's will. Much as I love her I now see her in a different perspective. Inside my beloved mother lurked a spark of fanaticism.

Unlike my mother, I believed absolutely that God's order of events could be altered. If I was to follow my mother's reasoning, there was nothing I could do with or in my life. I would not accept that. I would work out my destiny in the path best suited to my heart, feelings and intuition. For God bestowed on mankind the greatest, most sublime gift of all, freedom of will.

The thought of divorce became part of my life. I made no secret of it. I told Aron I would eventually leave him. He was not impressed. It was not only that he did not believe me; he simply could not visualize anyone taking a decisive step.

Meanwhile, however, it was my father who continued the subject of divorce; it was I who hesitated. Lurking in the back of my mind was the terrible fear that despite my father's understanding, he might yield to what he still viewed as a form of protection for me, the desire to marry me off again.

The years came and went, and the Depression continued on. The hopelessness became more accentuated. Men walked about idly, courageously fighting the feeling of defeat, which had overtaken them like an incurable disease. Yet the multitude survived. Relatives and old friends supported each other. They moved into homes together to help and to share.

Many in dire need of medical assistance had to apply to the outdoor clinics in hospitals. There the social-service workers added to their afflictions. Their attitude maimed the destitute, physically and mentally. There was little respect for the individual.

I had been suffering from inflamed eyelids which threatened to obstruct my vision. I could not bear to ask father for money to see an ophthalmologist, so I went to an outdoor clinic in one of our largest hospitals. I had to be interrogated by a social-service worker prior to being admitted to a doctor.

Here I was subjected to lengthy questioning followed by accusations, all pertaining to my monetary status. How difficult it was to tolerate! When I could bear no more and was preparing to leave without help, a man approached me. He said, "Please come with me, I will treat you in my private office free of charge." He had no doubt heard the conversation. He was a doctor of great skill. Treatment took some weeks, but he cured me and supplied the necessary medication. Furthermore, he insisted that I get in touch with him if my eye trouble recurred. I was deeply grateful. He had helped me physically and morally, restoring some of my faith in humanity.

My son Ari was taken ill with diphtheria. Terror and hopelessness overwhelmed me! I was well aware of conditions which existed in hospitals at that time and was by now familiar with what it meant to be poor and dependent upon public wards. Diphtheria was a contagious disease, and I had to consider the danger to my younger child. I was compelled to have my son hospitalized, a step I dreaded.

After two months I was permitted to bring my child home. I hoped to arrange some means of payment through the hospital. The dishonour I suffered! The most intimate details of our life were made public. I soon realized that the social-service worker knew she had found a victim. I was vulnerable; she could strike home with force. I was accused of hoarding money, of depriving others of care they sorely needed and of not discharging my duty to society. Throughout it all I insisted that my husband was unemployed, that I had no money. I was so humiliated that I refused to talk. They finally allowed me to take my child home.

I revere the memory of our compassionate pediatrician. How often, when he came to examine my children, he refused to accept a fee. He knew my impoverished position. Aside from that, he gave me samples of medicine under the pretence that he wanted them tested. I confided my difficulty concerning the hospital. He managed everything, and I did not pay at all.

The doctor was the son of a minister. There was never any question of Jew or Gentile between us. We were two people. Many were the discussions we had of our different faiths. There are people, who in their lifetime, cast their light upon their fellow men. It is a substance that warms us in the dark shivering hours of our lives.

Despite the Depression, changes were taking place. Help emerged for many under the name of "relief". Needy families were given relief money. Loans were made to home-owners and small businessmen enabling them to retain their homes and livelihoods. Those loans were later repaid, but at the time they were of immense help.

I recall with pain a scene I witnessed in our corner grocery shop. I had not abandonned my habit of studying the faces of those around me or making up stories about them. It helped me retain my sanity, I'm sure. A young woman looked with longing at each food product. It was as if, by eyeing the food, she tasted each delicious morsel. She wanted the memory of that taste to leave the shop with her. Although she was probably in her early thirties, she had a pinched look that gave her the appearance of a much older woman. It was her eyes, two pools of fear and indecision. In her purse she had her relief cheque which she fingered to make certain it was still there.

She lingered over each item as if it had the importance of life or death. The purchase of each article was a major decision. I saw her pick up an apple, replace it and select a smaller one. She picked up the larger apple again, then two smaller ones. With one hand holding the large apple and the other the two smaller ones, she weighed them lifting each hand like a scale. Finally she settled on the two small apples. They were added to her meagre purchases. My heart cried for her.

At times like this I experienced remorse that I had what I needed. It was not just that my parents sustained us. It was the manner in which it was done, as if I were doing *them* the favour. That, of course, is the great secret of giving, to give with grace so that the ones who receive are not mutilated in the process.

Here I was subjected to lengthy questioning followed by accusations, all pertaining to my monetary status. How difficult it was to tolerate! When I could bear no more and was preparing to leave without help, a man approached me. He said, "Please come with me, I will treat you in my private office free of charge." He had no doubt heard the conversation. He was a doctor of great skill. Treatment took some weeks, but he cured me and supplied the necessary medication. Furthermore, he insisted that I get in touch with him if my eye trouble recurred. I was deeply grateful. He had helped me physically and morally, restoring some of my faith in humanity.

My son Ari was taken ill with diphtheria. Terror and hopelessness overwhelmed me! I was well aware of conditions which existed in hospitals at that time and was by now familiar with what it meant to be poor and dependent upon public wards. Diphtheria was a contagious disease, and I had to consider the danger to my younger child. I was compelled to have my son hospitalized, a step I dreaded.

After two months I was permitted to bring my child home. I hoped to arrange some means of payment through the hospital. The dishonour I suffered! The most intimate details of our life were made public. I soon realized that the social-service worker knew she had found a victim. I was vulnerable; she could strike home with force. I was accused of hoarding money, of depriving others of care they sorely needed and of not discharging my duty to society. Throughout it all I insisted that my husband was unemployed, that I had no money. I was so humiliated that I refused to talk. They finally allowed me to take my child home.

I revere the memory of our compassionate pediatrician. How often, when he came to examine my children, he refused to accept a fee. He knew my impoverished position. Aside from that, he gave me samples of medicine under the pretence that he wanted them tested. I confided my difficulty concerning the hospital. He managed everything, and I did not pay at all.

The doctor was the son of a minister. There was never any question of Jew or Gentile between us. We were two people. Many were the discussions we had of our different faiths. There are people, who in their lifetime, cast their light upon their fellow men. It is a substance that warms us in the dark shivering hours of our lives.

Despite the Depression, changes were taking place. Help emerged for many under the name of "relief". Needy families were given relief money. Loans were made to home-owners and small businessmen enabling them to retain their homes and livelihoods. Those loans were later repaid, but at the time they were of immense help.

I recall with pain a scene I witnessed in our corner grocery shop. I had not abandonned my habit of studying the faces of those around me or making up stories about them. It helped me retain my sanity, I'm sure. A young woman looked with longing at each food product. It was as if, by eyeing the food, she tasted each delicious morsel. She wanted the memory of that taste to leave the shop with her. Although she was probably in her early thirties, she had a pinched look that gave her the appearance of a much older woman. It was her eyes, two pools of fear and indecision. In her purse she had her relief cheque which she fingered to make certain it was still there.

She lingered over each item as if it had the importance of life or death. The purchase of each article was a major decision. I saw her pick up an apple, replace it and select a smaller one. She picked up the larger apple again, then two smaller ones. With one hand holding the large apple and the other the two smaller ones, she weighed them lifting each hand like a scale. Finally she settled on the two small apples. They were added to her meagre purchases. My heart cried for her.

At times like this I experienced remorse that I had what I needed. It was not just that my parents sustained us. It was the manner in which it was done, as if I were doing *them* the favour. That, of course, is the great secret of giving, to give with grace so that the ones who receive are not mutilated in the process.

Over the years I tried to make up somehow to my parents for their bounty to me. Daily I was at their home to help in any way possible. There were papers to translate, trips to the bank and the post office, telephone messages as well as standing by during the emergencies which occur always in a rabbi's home. I continued in my role of father's *shammes*, as he lovingly called me.

We had happier moments. Father's income was augmented by marriages he performed at home. A witness to many weddings reposed in a corner of father's study. It was the *chuppa*, a canopy under which the wedding ceremony was performed. Four sturdy rods supported it. Failing someone better, I often held up one of the rods. If that service were not required of me, I had another. I played the piano to the tune of *"Chusan, Kalleh, Mazel Tov"* (groom and bride, good luck).

Most of the marriages performed in father's study had one common factor. The participants were poor — they could not afford a synagogue wedding. My parents had a special warmth for those who had few relatives. Often the couple arrived alone. Father would smile and assure the couple that the future was theirs to shape. Then he would turn to us and say, "The bride is comely. The groom will rejoice with her." If the bride happened to be plain, father would sigh and say, "Mercifully, the marriage will be consummated in the dark."

---

My beloved father became ill. He developed a heart condition that was to endure for years. At the time we did not realize how blessed we were that father lived seven years after his first attack. While the ailment impaired, it did not incapacitate him. He needed the gravest care, and we gave it to him with devotion. We seemed to live in a glass house that could collapse about us and leave us destitute and alone.

At first the attacks were frequent, and our hearts stood still. Mother ministered to him. She was constantly at his side. It was remarkable how she dealt with these assaults. She had developed an inner sense over the years of knowing exactly what to do. Most of all she called out to him, pleading with him not to leave her, that she needed him, willing him to live, and above all, telling how much she loved him. He responded. It was a technique inspired by love.

As his illness intensified and developed to a more dangerous stage, I became obsessed with the urge to see him more often. Each day, as I left my parents' home, I quietly opened the door of father's study to bid him good night. My eyes lingered on his dear face with pain and longing. I wanted his features to inscribe themselves on my heart and on my mind so that I could keep him with me forever.

He would glance up from his writing, sadness showing in his eyes, and say, "Leah, why do you look at me so intently?" We both knew the answer.

Then a new phase of our lives opened. Father spoke about leaving Montreal. He had purchased land in Palestine and began to speak of a home in Jerusalem. He had also been informed that the chief rabbi of

Palestine was to retire, and there were indications that father might be invited to replace him.

There was never any doubt that my children and I would leave for Palestine with my parents. We avoided the question of divorce by mutual consent. Documents were already being prepared for our departure.

When father spoke about Jerusalem, his face lit up with a sublime joy that defies description. Palestine was woven into his being, not like a fine thread, rather a strong rope that encased his very body and soul. Sadly it was not to be! Moses did not enter the Promised Land, nor did my father! Our papers arrived six weeks after his death.

Through the years of father's illness, he went about his life in a normal manner. He served the community and continued his writing. He understood his sickness and met each setback in a rational way.

With the decision to leave Montreal, activity began in my father's study. He started taking count of his vast library. Mother, Israel and I were alarmed although we did not voice our concern in words. Father bundled up packages of *sphorim* which he labelled. He put his papers in order. There seemed to be a finality in that procedure; it was more like a farewell. Father was pale and tense, but mercifully he would often rally and become his hopeful self again.

While we were watching and protecting father, we failed to detect the mounting stress in mother. The doctors who paid such close attention to father never once suggested that they examine mother. We did not know that her blood pressure was so high.

A catastrophe descended on us — my beloved mother suffered a stroke! That was the first and only time I saw father lose control. He was enveloped in fear and anguish. Within minutes two doctors arrived and mother was rushed to a hospital. I turned the other way as I saw father watching and weeping at the window as the ambulance drove mother away.

The following morning father and I went to the hospital. We were not permitted to see her. As we sat in the lobby debating what course to follow, a prominent Jewish physician noticed us. He asked if he could be of service. He was truly a godsend for, after that, we were allowed to visit mother at any time. She did not recognize us. She was able to speak but only incoherently. She could walk. A nurse told us mother had gotten up from her bed, insisting it was time to kindle the Sabbath candles. Wherever she went, God went with her.

Actually, it was a mild stroke, and we were soon able to take her home. Father so dearly wanted her to be with him. He seldom left her bedside. He nursed her with untiring devotion and attended to her physical needs. When I protested, he said, "Leah, that is my privilege as a devoted husband."

In a few weeks mother showed marked improvement. Father roused her from lethargy and the stupor she was in. Mostly he would not permit her to sleep. He talked incessantly to her, and she reacted favourably.

During the brief period Mother was hospitalized, she developed a bedsore. It was very painful. Father cured it with soothing ointments of his own prescription, which he applied gently. Chia and I watched in wonder as he lifted that awful sore piece by piece. My father was endowed with many gifts.

Chia was a most devoted daughter. She came to Montreal often to assist with the nursing. I helped father run the house and gradually took over much of the care of mother. She was now able to walk and had recovered her mental faculties. Her mind was as sharp as ever.

A task I took upon myself was to bathe mother. She could not climb into a tub, so I placed her on towels and washed her. It became a ceremony every Friday before the Sabbath. At first she was embarrassed to appear naked before me. I pretended not to notice. She was close to seventy, and her body was still soft and beautiful. She would watch me, and her face would light up with love and gratitude. She wore a silk cap which replaced the *shaytl* that had become too heavy. I dressed her in light-weight clothes to insure comfort. After I completed her bath ritual, I would lead her to father and place her hand in his. I treasure those memories.

On one such occasion she began to cry. She looked at me and said, "See how much trouble I am to you." I replied, "Really, Mother, you have a short memory. Did you not bathe and nurse me when I was a baby?" Whereupon, I took the nipples of her breasts in my mouth and suckled them. She began to laugh and cry and heaped many blessings on me.

Father's illness had a devastating affect on mother. She was dogmatic in her religious beliefs. While she accepted all happenings as God's will, she would not resign herself to father's sickness and the inevitable fact of his passing. It was impossible to tell her to count her blessings and be grateful for the many wonderful years she had shared with father. I had the same feelings. We wanted father to live forever.

Father had suffered one of his most severe heart attacks. He was propped up in bed. My habit was to sit on his bed and gently stroke his hands. The inevitable questions always followed the attacks. "Tell me about my children and my grandchildren. What are they doing now?" So, I would name each child, how many children they had and what they were doing now. Father speculated on their futures. He was well aware that soon he would part from his loved ones. It was akin to an ethereal feeling from which he could not take complete leave. He longed for a spiritual vision of his children and grandchildren to imprint itself eternally on his heart and soul. His gaze lingered on my mother's face, then on mine as if to seal an agreement between us that mother would be with me.

After that particular onslaught, he surprised us by analysing the character of each of his children. He left me out. I touched his beard to attract his attention. "Father, I too am a child of yours. Why did you leave me out?" His eyes held a whimsical smile, "True, but you are Leah!" Perhaps that was a greater compliment.

I was concerned with mother's state of health. She spoke often of the way that children neglect their parents. She repeated the story that one mother can care for ten children, but ten children cannot take care of one mother or father. Her fear was that she would be deserted after father passed away.

The year was 1935, the month was October and the weather remained warm and pleasant. The leaves with their radiant colours were scattered about. The fall is truly reminiscent of old age—that glorious season when the turning of the leaves is like our declining years.

It was Simchat Torah. I yielded to the request of Aron's parents and agreed to spend that joyous festival with them. We were surprised when Ari refused to visit Aron's parents with us. It turned into a memorable incident. My older son began to cry and sob. He kept insisting that he had to see his *zaide* before we left. Aron was obliged to take him to vist my father. That was the last time the child saw his grandfather.

I was in daily contact with my parents. They did not lift a telephone receiver on festivals or on the Sabbath. I waited until sunset to telephone. There was no reply. I called a neighbour who told me that father had been taken ill and was in the Jewish General Hospital. My world collapsed.

I rushed to my mother's side. She explained what had happened. Every year on Simchat Torah, my parents gave a *Kiddush* which consisted of hosting the members of the congregation who escorted father home. After partaking of the wine and plentiful good food, it was the custom for the men to clap hands and demand, "Torah, Torah." Father responded with Torah discourse, after which would follow the Chassidic dancing.

It was while father spoke that he suffered a fatal stroke. It was befitting that my father, who lived by the teachings of the Law, should expire with the words of the Law on his tongue! Although he passed away on the third day after he had suffered the stroke, he really died on Simchat Torah. He was seventy-five years of age.

Mother, Israel and I spent those three precious days at father's bedside. He lost his speech but was in control of the rest of his faculties. He knew where he was, and what had happened to him. His eyes were eloquent. The three of us took turns feeding him liquids. He lay there like a lion for he was a king, a king of our people and a king of men!

Israel did not seem to grasp the tragic reality of the moment. He did not want to believe that father could die. He wandered in and out of the room with quiet despair. The leaders of father's congregation had watched Israel grow from boyhood to manhood. They tried to console mother and, directing themselves to my brother, said, "Our great and beloved rabbi is now leaving us. We are desolate. With us, your father will live forever, for you will take his place!"

Doctors lined up outside the sick room and waited their turn to pay homage with their last look at my father. There was a hush and a poignant sadness encircling the hospital floor. We shared a common thought. When, if ever, will there emerge a man like father?

There were no death throes, no death rattles. We stood at his bedside, and father seemed to be sleeping. Suddenly he opened his eyes. There was no fear in them, no surprise, just acceptance. He glanced up as though he saw someone well-known to him. His eyes gazed upwards, and I felt compelled to cast my eyes in the same direction, but I saw no one. I turned back to father, saw him gently close his eyes, and he was no more!

I have lived through harrowing, soul-searing events in my life but the passing of my father left me the most vulnerable. I pleaded with my brothers and sisters gathered to bid farewell to father, who lay on the floor of his study, that we prevent his being interred. "Let us keep him," I begged.

Outside the street was crowded. Most Jewish businesses, large and small, were closed for the day. Many tried to make their way into our home to pick up mementos of father. The police were waiting on motorcycles to escort the crowds to the funeral. Newspapers, foreign and domestic, bore one sentence: "A LIGHT HAS GONE OUT IN ISRAEL!" But even more, a light had gone out in my heart.

CHAPTER 10

 *Divorce
and the
Aftermath*

AFTER FATHER PASSED AWAY, I moved permanently
into my parents' home. I had lived there most of my
life anyway, and there was never any question as to
who would look after mother.

We settled into a nervous calm. Israel and I realized it was a race
against time for mother. Neither of us was too hopeful. Mother talked
continuously of father, and who could blame her? In a sense my
mother's life ended with father's death. There was a difference in our
grief. I accepted father's death and went on with my life; mother did
not.

Even the fact that Israel, one of my mother's sons, had at last become
an ordained rabbi was of little solace to my mother. While my father
was still in the hospital, and the heads of the community knew it was
only a matter of time, Israel was offered father's position, which he
refused. Mother was displeased with Israel's decision.

Israel had become betrothed to Sophia, the daughter of a *rebbe*, shortly before father's death, and a wedding date had been set. After father's death mother wanted my brother to bring his bride to live with us. I was firmly against it. I knew mother was dictatorial, accustomed to having her way. It was now even more difficult for her to relinquish power. Also mother and Sophia did not take to each other. Sophia had another name which was Sarah; mother's name was also Sarah. There is a Jewish superstition that when such similarity of names occurs, it hastens the death of the older person.

Israel left for New York where the wedding was to take place. Mother was to follow later. I became anxious as I watched mother. It seemed she was walking slowly, and her speech came haltingly. A few days before the trip, she dropped a cup. I put her to bed. I stayed up all night watching her. She was fast asleep, and her face was deeply flushed. I could not wake her.

In the morning the doctor informed me that mother had suffered a massive stroke — paralysis on one side, the lower part of her body lifeless and complete loss of speech. I told myself that mother would recover; it simply could not happen to one so forceful and vibrant. The doctors just looked at me pityingly. It was mother's second stroke and hopeless.

The battle began to keep mother clean. My sisters urged me to call in a nurse. After a few days I came to an important realization. Money! It struck me with brutal force that through the years my parents had not accumulated any financial reserves. Father had invested in land in Israel, and otherwise there was only a little over 1000 dollars. I clung to that tenaciously; it had to last. The doctors had warned me that a stroke victim either went right away like my father or lingered for years. There would be no improvement.

I did not listen to that. I engaged the services of a trained attendant to massage my mother's body and arms. I bought a hospital bed and wheel chair, which I took around the house to keep mother's mind in touch with the house. I sat her facing a window so she could look out and see life around her. I refused to allow her to stagnate. I enlisted the aid of my children. Each day they would approach their grandmother and embrace her and talk to her. The children were wonderful, and I think she understood. The attention they paid their grandmother helped keep her mind alive for a long time.

I asked my siblings to contribute a small amount each week so I could hire some help, for they soon tired of coming. No assistance was forthcoming, and we quarrelled bitterly. They had one solution, "Give mother away." I had one reply, "Over my dead body."

I shuddered to think what old-age homes were like during the time mother was ill. At one period I did place my mother in a nursing home. The next day when I visited her, she would not look at me. I immediately took her back home.

I decided to appeal for help from the Jewish Community Council. The Council was a religious body and not in the business of catering to the needy. Regardless, I called the Council and asked for an appointment.

I was called into the hall where the elders of the Council were gathered. Not for a moment had I thought of what I would say. Still I had to speak.

"You are aware that my mother is hopelessly ill. I am here to ask — please I emphasize at the start, not to beg, but to ask — for a pension for my mother. My mother is not a *nebech* (someone to be pitied). I have asked my brothers and sisters for money; they told me to put mother into an institution. I cannot do that. Mother cannot talk, but her mind is still clear. So you may dismiss my request and say the duty lies with the children, and you would be within your rights to say so.

"Now my father served the community very well. But that is what he wanted out of life. So you can say that if my father enjoyed his life work, you owe his widow nothing. And you may be right.

"I unfortunately have no money. The only contribution I can make to my mother is to care for her. So what I need is a pension for her, which I cannot compel you to give. Do I have a right to ask that of you? I think I do. It would be a repayment for my father's services. But you have a right to refuse. I fervently hope you will not do so, that you will grant the pension to my mother. Even willingly and with grace."

No one interrupted me, no one inquired if father had left money. When I finished speaking, I was asked to wait in the outer office. They would discuss my request. I do not think even five minutes passed, before I was called in.

"We will be pleased to give your mother a pension. Furthermore, we want to impress upon you that you are to call on us for further help, or in any emergency that you may encounter." And so it was mother received her pension regularly, and a great help it was.

I prefer to let those years lie dormant. As the years passed, I became more weary. I ranted and raved against my brothers and sisters. I had learned enough about nursing to look after mother well, but I cried and implored God to put an end to her living death. I wanted the mother I loved to die! I raged within myself. I know those years were hard on Aron. And on my children. I was harassed, overworked and often despondent. I had so little time for my children.

I constantly wonder what constitutes our duty to our parents. What does it involve? Was I right to keep mother home? My sisters and brothers thought otherwise. Were they in the right, or was I their conscience? Would I choose to suffer the same ordeal again? Yes I would for I believe my mother was far better off at home. Her mind remained clear, and her home was where she belonged.

Somehow I retained my sanity, such as it was. What helped me was the writing of a series of short stories about my father: "I Pay a Visit to the Beloved Rabbi". It proved an outlet for me; my father came to life and I did what I enjoyed most, which was to write. The articles first appeared in *The Canadian Jewish Review*, then went on to an American magazine, *The Jewish Spectator*.

It was a living death for seven years. My wonderful mother lived in the throes of agony and anguish — unable to speak, having to endure a helplessness and dependency she had always dreaded. I remember that heart-rending prayer she had so often recited, "God do not desert me in my old age," as if she could foresee the future. But through it all my mother remained beautiful. In 1942 seven years after my father's death, my lovely mother died.

After my mother passed away, I began taking stock of my life. Financially things had improved. Aron's father was doing well, so Aron benefited. Aron had remained with his father; that had ceased to bother me long before. The assistance I had received from my parents through the years had always included Aron. Now he was able to take care of himself. I was very happy for him and for myself, for that gave me a sense of freedom and the hope of eventual release. A new life beckoned.

But more than ever I was beset by loneliness. During those difficult years of my mother's illness, I had abandoned all thoughts of divorce. Now I contemplated it again. The hunger for companionship was uppermost in my mind. I had a need, a longing to share my thoughts, to converse, to air my views of books and plays I had experienced. It was almost a torment. Desolation gripped me like a vise. I was pursued by my own needs.

My sons were now teen-agers, I had leisure time, and I began to attend lectures. The Jewish library offered courses in Talmud. And so I met Reuben. We became acquainted at lectures. He was intelligent, talkative and charming, well versed in Mosaic Law and extremely well-read. I find it unbelievable, but if I encountered him now I would not recognize him. I sometimes wonder if I invented him. It is no longer of any importance. It is like a storm that came and quietly passed. It did not leave a wreck.

Nor is it of any consequence that the relationship did not endure. I was neither bruised nor maimed. Certainly I felt pain and even despair when it ended. But for me it served a great purpose. I experienced a love for which I felt an urgent need. It was part of living. Indeed it was a fulfilment for which I was grateful. I lived through an event, and while Eve ate from the tree of knowledge, I partook of the tree of love.

My moral sense would not allow me both to live with a husband and have an affair. I had wanted a divorce for years. Now it meant that it transpired sooner. Of course, there was gossip and condemnation. Aron took it hard. He never once admitted that I had been telling him for years that our marriage would have to end. He now tried his utmost to please me and hold on. I found it amusing that I had suddenly become desirable. As for his father, he acted as if I was actually divorcing *him*.

Aron's father immediately set about the details of the divorce. Then he had second thoughts. He arranged for an American rabbi to persuade me to reconsider. "All will be forgiven," the rabbi told me. "You have not been much of a wife, Leah. Go through with the divorce, and doors will be closed to you forever." I wondered if he was referring to the Willensky doors to Paradise. I was supposed to be frightened; actually I was angry. Not once was there reference to any differences between Aron and myself, nor to the hard times I had gone through, nor to the help I had to accept from my parents, nor that I was penniless after years of marriage. I had absolutely nothing.

I received a *get*, and my marriage was annulled. It was a period when annulments were easier to procure than civil divorces. My sons, now thirteen and eighteen, proceeded to inform me that they had become illegitimate. Furthermore Moshe, who received support from his father, advised me to treat him with deference or he would leave home. Despite our worries, we were still able to laugh.

Divorce is like major surgery — to be performed only when life is in danger. However, the patient undergoing such operation must be in condition to withstand the uncertainty. I grew, but it was a long, dreary, agonizing process. For years I had been sheltered by my parents. All my thinking was influenced by them and emanated from one source, the Jewish one. Now the battle for survival began. I had no money, but that was nothing new. The fight was prolonged by the stark reality that I was not trained for any job. This proved a tragedy in my life. Despite the love my parents bore me, they failed to prepare me for life in the outside world — all the more regrettable since I had the potential and the will.

The first step I took was to assure a home for myself and my children. I had a flat on St. Urbain Street that we had moved into during my mother's illness. So I rented out some rooms and that gave me a bit of money. Now I had to find work.

Soon I perceived that the prospects for work were not good. Through money loaned to me, I opened a boarding house in Ste-Agathe in the Laurentians. It was terribly hard work. Most painful was the fact that I had to be assisted by my sons. They worked with me unstintingly; they gave me their support and their love. Never will I be able to repay them, no matter how long I may live! In the end I was forced to give that up. I repaid the loan, and my children and I set about repairing the damage. I began job hunting in earnest and managed to find quite a few. But they were all very strenuous and had no future. I worked in a laundry, in a bakery; I looked after underprivileged children; I worked and I worked. Meanwhile I was determined to find employment where I could remain, learn and progress. I vowed not to lose faith in myself and deteriorate.

I cannot bear to recount the rebuffs, the disdainful refusals, the broken promises. One job I applied for was in a bookshop. The owner, a middle-aged man, looked me up and down as if I was a race horse. He was obviously impressed; he offered me the job and his bed.

I recall vividly one particular day in my life. I was out looking for a job. I had spent two precious car tickets in my search. There was no job and no more tickets. I sat down on the curb and looked in both directions to decide which one to take. I must have sat there for a long time. I reviewed in my mind the various jobs at which I had worked, and then I became angry. I decided to have a one-sided argument with God. "I will not tolerate the treatment I am receiving. In case you don't know who I am, I am Leah, and when I was born, a place in this world was allotted to me. I want that place. I will not be deprived of my place, and I intend to fight for it." I had made my case clear and felt better. God did not throw down a car ticket, and I walked a long way home. But my spirit was revived.

While the job hunting continued, I soon realized that I absolutely could not find employment without sacrificing the Sabbath and the Jewish festivals. I was not concerned with the salary. Wherever I went, I offered to accept a smaller wage if I could be let off for the Sabbath. It did not work, so in addition to the arduous task of job hunting, I now had to face the dilemma of my principles.

There was more at stake than the observance of the Sabbath. I had to reassess my values. Did my upbringing restrict me or did it enlarge my mental capacity? Would I be giving up precious values if I did not observe the Sabbath, or would I be freer or happier if I did give them up? I had to work out my own philosophy, to evaluate what my roots meant to me. Were they deep enough to protect me in the decision I had to make? I had entered a different world, no longer an observer, but a participant. I became obsessed by the fear that desecrating the Sabbath was the first step to what I termed "destruction-assimilation". I wondered which offered more in life, adherence to tradition or freedom from it.

Soon I realized that what I had been taught about the beauty of Jewish life did not hinder me, nor did the observance or non-observance of the Sabbath mar it. My values did not change; they mellowed. A keener sense emerged within me. I now knew that I would ever be guided by the roots I had acquired in my childhood. These roots had given me a heritage and had shaped me not only as a Jew but as a person as well. And when I could see myself both as a Jew and a person, I could define myself as liberated. I could embrace my life without abandoning my immigrant roots nor my beloved Chassidism. I could combine the old and the new, without sacrificing either. Indeed, one would serve to enhance the other.

Meanwhile I had yet to clarify in my mind the problem of working on the Sabbath. True, it was out of necessity, but that did not absolve me. I had to make a truce with myself which entailed a compromise. I hoped time would bring a measure of security that would enable me to return to observance. I realized that while observance is an integral part of Judaism, Jewish life does not hinge on it. Judaism is a consecration of the soul and the spirit, while observance is like an outer garment. Its purpose acts to keep the inner faith warm and vibrant so that the flame does not dim.

The job hunting continued. It was a battle but I was still comparatively young. Although in my early middle age, I had strength and stamina. When I was born, the angels who endowed the newborn dozed off when beauty was doled out, but they made up for it with courage. I had that all right. And what was most important, I nourished a belief in myself. I knew I was capable, so there had to be a place for me; I was determined to find it.

I answered an ad from a night club. I had composed a letter of reference naming a firm I had worked for. The owner of the club read the letter and asked who had written it. I admitted that I had. He gave me the job.

I now loved my work. The work offered scope; it was interesting and challenging. I was able to make rapid progress. I enrolled in a business school to learn bookkeeping and typing. I approached my subjects with a ferocity that alarmed my instructors. At work I had been hired to enter the customer checks on a sheet which had to balance. Soon I answered the telephones. I graduated from the reservations to arranging banquets and dinners for organizations. That brought business to the club. Next I looked after the publicity and assisted in a radio program we had. My salary was increased, and I was given the keys to various departments and a gun since I handled money entrusted to me from some side business in which my employers indulged.

After several years at the club, television came and night clubs suffered. After the club I found a job with a baby-furniture firm. I remained there close to eighteen years. I suppose I had what was a unique method of selling. I told the truth about merchandise and never sold a product to a customer who could not afford to buy it. My employer insisted I would ruin him and would land him in the poorhouse, where I promised to visit him. He would bemoan the fact that he ever hired me. But it was this man who enabled me to buy a home. He arranged for a loan of 5000 dollars at the bank for which he signed. In return I promised to stay with him as long as I worked. We remained great friends.

When my employer gave me the welcome news that he would guarantee a 5000 dollar loan for me at the bank, I was elated. My goal was to buy a property and establish a rooming house. This would furnish me with a home and security for my old age. It was a logical solution for a woman advanced in years. Eventually I would not be forced to go out to work.

I began to look for a property. I called an agent, and we arranged a meeting. The first house he showed me turned out to be exactly what I wanted. I told the agent I was prepared to make an offer. "You have seen the house only once," he exclaimed. "Yes, but I am looking at what the house will be like after I work on it," was my reply.

The house I bought had seven rooms, a garage and a garden. It was in a deplorable condition. The rooms and hall were painted a dismal blue. The garage floor had sunk to a dangerous state. First I fumigated the house; then I painted it a bright yellow and white.

A rooming house is ideal for a woman my age. Only, never let it be said that it is easy. I worked very hard and often had to deal with alcoholics, deviants and other unusual people. It was almost impossible to judge who would be a good lodger and who wouldn't. A young man, smelling like a rose, never took garbage out — he simply threw it under the bed. Another young man had a devout Catholic grandmother who telephoned me every Sunday morning to awaken her grandson for Mass. After a few Sundays I told her there would be a charge for the wake-up service. She never called back. Another lodger was an alcoholic lady who persisted in getting into the bathtub from which she was unable to emerge.

The greatest difficulty with being a landlady of a rooming house is drawing the line in dealing with lodgers. One likes to be friendly and hospitable; then come the dangers of too close contact, being taken advantage of and trouble.

At one point I had two rooms joined, installed a bathroom and rented it as an apartment. The first occupant was a young lady named Marie. She was not French; she just cultivated an accent. She worked as a lab technician. Marie was angular, tall and plain. But she had innumerable men friends. If she had sex appeal, as far as I was concerned, that attraction was concealed in a place not visible. I began to wonder how she kept track of them. We were friendly, so one day over coffee I ventured to ask, "Marie, please, how is it you have so many men friends? What puzzles me most is how you keep track of them."

"Well, the reason I have many," was the reply, "is that I am experimenting sexually to see which method suits me most."

"All right, fine. Only judging from the number, how do you remember who is who and which method each uses? Do you keep a record?"

"Why, I never thought of that. That's what I'll do from now on."

It so happened that immediately thereafter Marie broke a leg skiing. I thought the system was doomed. I would never find out which method was the right one. Marie was in bed for two weeks. I went upstairs with trays, not forgetting the four o'clock snacks. This went on for two weeks, and I realized those trays were too appetizing; Marie might spend the rest of her life in bed.

One morning I told Marie I would deliver her tray earlier as I had to go out. I ascended, knocked on her door — no reply. I always carried the keys, so I opened the door. There was Marie in bed with experiment number seventeen. I all but dropped the tray. Undaunted, both glanced at me and laughed. At lunch time I asked Marie how it was accomplished with a broken leg. "Simple," she said, "it was just another experiment!"

In a large room upstairs, I had as a lodger, a Lithuanian girl. We struck up a friendship that lasted long after she left my house. This girl, a young woman in her thirties, was unmarried. She was a buxom blond and very strong. She had a tendency to move furniture around in my living room. I never asked her to do so, but it made no difference. She moved things anyway. Every Sunday Olga would come down and cook supper. She was an excellent cook and had worked in a kosher home. The first Christmas she was in my house, she asked me to accompany her to Mass which I did.

Then one day Olga brought a young man home. Soon they became engaged, and we planned the wedding. There was a ceremony after which the guests gathered in my living room. With the help of a friend, we prepared sandwiches and brewed coffee. Olga had bought a bottle of champagne which she guarded with her life. It had been hidden in her cupboard. I handed each guest a glass and Olga went to her room to fetch the precious bottle. Olga poured the liquor; we prepared to drink. As we tasted the champagne, horror struck us. Someone had stolen into Olga's room, emptied the liquor and replaced it with urine! Well, we never forgot that wedding.

My lodgers did not change often, although I occasionally had to dispose of one. That was not easy — it was easier to find a lodger, than to dismiss a lodger. I learned that the hard way. Necessity had cautioned me to face the possibility of danger. I soon learned never to walk in front of a stranger.

A lodger in the house, a young woman, had become troublesome by her continual arguments with other lodgers. Because I maintained peace at all costs, I requested her to move. It was while I was on my way down the stairs that she came behind me. Fortunately there were just a few steps left, but she pushed me down and then gave me a severe beating. I went to the police. From my description they recognized her, and she was arrested. She already had a record. There was a trial, and I had to be present. She was sentenced to several weeks in jail.

There were lighter moments in my rooming house that compensated for the dangerous, unpleasant ones. I had a lodger in his early sixties who moved about like a shadow. I called him "the Phantom". I was in the habit of giving names to my lodgers that served to identify them while they lived in my house. In this way I could describe and talk about them to my grandchildren who were so often amused by my tales. Long after they had left, I could not remember their real names, but I always remembered the names I had given them. I was anxious to have the Phantom move; he had been in my house over a year, and as time passed he developed fawning ways towards me that I found irritating. I began to think of an excuse to get rid of him and fate played into my hands.

I had observed that all rooming houses around me had a set of rules posted in their hallways. I had refrained from rules, only hanging a card in each room asking that the room be kept clean and the rent paid in advance. I could have spared the effort; an honourable lodger needed no rules. Still there was one stipulation that did not embrace honour, just sex. I decided to enforce an overall rule: my lodgers' friends of the opposite sex had to be out of the house by eleven o'clock. This rule required some vigilance. Late one night I heard loud voices from the Phantom's room. There was so much noise that I discreetly knocked on the door saying that the lady had to leave. I could hear the lady ask, "Who is that?"

"It's my landlady," the Phantom replied in a quavering voice. "Tell her to shut up," replied the lady. "Oh, you don't understand. My landlady is Jewish."

"Jewish?" came a swift reply. "Give her two dollars." Hear O Israel, I thought. The Jewish religion is now worth two dollars. The matter did not end there. "No, that won't do. It's worse. Her father was a rabbi." From the lady, "You mean he was in the government?"

"No, a rabbi is like a priest."

"A priest!" she shrieked. "I am getting out of here." The next day, the Phantom left for good.

I had rented a room to a lady in her late forties. An extremely handsome woman, she had luxuriant wavy red hair and was very well endowed. She soon acquainted me with her life story—a husband who beat her, various lovers, an inheritance stolen from her. Her story was all mixed up, and soon I was too. I just kept agreeing and watching the clock. I knew she went to work at certain unusually late hours. Soon she began bringing her gentleman friends in to spend the nights. So I called her downstairs and reminded her of the rules regarding men in her room, and she began to protest. "This is my room and I have the right to do what I like as long as I pay my rent. Furthermore, I intend to stay here as long as I like."

She also kept repeating what a nice man her friend was and how jealous her friends were because he was such a good "catch". An idea struck me. I knew it was mad, but madness and I were not strangers. I would try it.

The next time her friend spent the night, I invited them both for breakfast, I directed myself to the man and asked sweetly what he would like for breakfast. I plied him with pancakes and freshly brewed coffee. Then I talked about how rich I was and how I would like a man like him. It worked. She never allowed him to come back, and she left the next week.

PART FIVE

CHAPTER 11

# Journeys
# to the
# Present

THE ROOMING HOUSE was now sufficiently lucrative
to open a new vista for me which my children
helped realize financially. My greatest dream had
always been to travel. I longed to become
acquainted with the cultures of other countries. My children knew
this, so as soon as they could afford it, they sent me off.

My first trip in the 1950s was to London to visit my younger son,
who had decided to pursue his writing career to better advantage in
England. I travelled by ship on the Cunard line. Until I boarded the
ship, I never for a moment believed that I was really going. Ever since
that first momentous trip, I have never lost the feeling of excitement
pulsating through me whenever I travel. For me, it is an incredible
thrill to be able to travel, to have the means after all my years of
deprivation. I am humble in my thanks; it is a miracle!

Before I left for London, Ari arrived with my luggage. I stood on deck waving good-bye to him, just as I had so often seen on the film screen. I felt like a movie star. The ship fascinated me. I roamed around the decks. In my cabin I stood at the porthole looking at the vastness of the ocean. In my mind rose the image of the ship which had carried me and my family to Canada. I recalled that first ocean crossing. I had not been seasick on that journey, and now it was the same. I remembered how I walked holding on to ropes, and I looked in the corners for the little immigrant girl I had been. I thought of my arduous voyage through life, and I was besieged by memories.

As the ship drew near England, I asked myself, what did I expect to derive from this trip, aside from the satisfaction that I was at last able to travel at all? True, there was ever the thirst for knowledge, to keep learning, developing and growing. But at my age it was also time for reflection, and in a sense my trips became the culmination of my life. I was now my own person.

When I arrived, it was very exciting for me to see my younger son, from whom it had been difficult for me to separate. Love surged over me when I saw Moshe's face. He had acquired a maturity, a greater depth. We both had attained a measure of success. He was in London where he had aspired to be and was working hard at his writing. And I was face to face with a culture I had read about for years. But best of all, I was walking beside him.

Moshe took me to the most interesting places in London. I entered a cultural world completely separate from my Jewish one. Through my son, I met fascinating people — artists, writers, actors, actresses. And while I made comparisons between my Jewishness and other philosophies, my mind was broadened, and I accepted others as they were. I had become more flexible.

My next trip followed close behind. Russia had always intrigued me. For decades it had been the home of multitudes of Jews and the seat of the great *yeshivas* of Europe. More recently it had become a hotbed of anti-Semitism. For me personally, it was the place where my brother Baruch had been murdered, and where his daughter Shoshana now lived.

In 1932 at the age of seventeen, Shoshana and her mother and brother had returned to "utopia" Russia. Yet, father felt, she was not lost to us. "The time will come when Baruch's child will claim her relationship with us. We must not fail her." Father continued, "If it is too late for mother and me, Leah, it will be up to you. When you find her, please give her a message. Acquaint her with the heritage her father bequeathed to her. Tell her not to betray it. And above all, tell her how much her father loved her." So father left me with a legacy — to find Shoshana. It was a search I conducted for many years.

Ultimately, father was right. The time arrived when my niece made frantic efforts to reach us, but it was too late for my parents. As an Intourist (the travel service of the Russian government) guide she had the opportunity to meet many Canadian visitors. I later found out that when she met them, she always made the same plea, "My grandfather is a rabbi in Montreal. Please tell him that I am alive. Tell my grandmother, tell Leah."

One day a man who had visited Russia telephoned. He gave me a message from Shoshana and mailed a handkerchief to me. Shoshana and I corresponded for a time. I managed to mail two parcels to her. Then years of silence. I was overburdened with my own problems. I forgot her, I remembered her, I tried to locate her. I gave up and tried again. Many years passed.

Since to the family I was still *shammes*, they often asked me if I had found Shoshana. Then, the miracle! One day Chia's eldest daughter asked the inevitable query, "Have you located Shoshana?" Then, "I don't know what you will make of it, but I must tell you this story. One evening I attended a lecture and met a Jewish writer who mentioned that he had heard from an old girl friend in Russia. Something the writer said struck me, and I asked whether his girl friend came from Montreal, and did she have a family there? The reply was, 'At one time she had grandparents. The grandfather was a well-known rabbi.'"

I lost no time and immediately wrote for the address of the person I hoped was my niece. I still was not certain. When I acquired the information, I sent a letter to Russia. Soon thereafter, a letter from Shoshana arrived. I telephoned her. She was hysterically happy, unable to make sense. She had a daughter who spoke to me also.

The next day I went to the Russian consulate to apply for a visa. It took several months till I received my Russian visa. I had decided on a private one which would enable me to stay with Shoshana instead of in a hotel. I knew my niece would be my best guide.

Shoshana and I wrote weekly before my trip. But I did not know what kind of person she really was. Letters that passed between us were superficial, for we were afraid mail would be opened and read by the Russian government. I was apprehensive about our meeting. I did not want the same treatment from my niece that my parents suffered from her mother. Nor did I want recriminations or bitterness on either side. I was determined that nothing should mar our reunion. I was deeply concerned, for I felt I was on a mission for my parents. I longed to convey this to Shoshana. I fervently hoped that the spark of Jewishness was alive somewhere in my niece. I had no right to alter Shoshana's views, but I felt I was the voice of Baruch, her father, and had to deliver a message. After that my niece could react in the way she wished; her life was her own.

We were reunited in Moscow. There stood Shoshana with her grown daughter waiting for me. There was no embarrassment in our meeting, only love! We cried and we laughed and we rejoiced and we spoke of our departed loved ones. And I offered a vote of thanks to the God of my fathers. It was a great day!

Since Shoshana was conversant with the history of Russia, its countless historical locations and museums, we spent day after day visiting these places. I marvelled at the wonderful Bolshoi Ballet where I was fortunate to see the greatest performers. I attended an opera and sat in the Czar's box. I kept telling Shoshana that any minute we might be mistaken for the Czar and knifed. Symphony halls and theatres were open to all. In the audience I saw aged Russians who had never entered a concert hall, now able to view these arts. That was commendable. The museums were also accessible and always crowded for the admission fees were insignificant. I was most impressed by the wonderful Russian paintings. They were, like the works of the Russian writers — dramatic, poignant and very beautiful.

It was my habit that in each foreign city, I visited a synagogue. This was not simple in Russia. We finally found a beautiful, spacious synagogue on a small street in Moscow. The synagogue was crowded; I looked at the worshippers. I searched for younger Jews but most of them were older. The few young people present were composed of the K.G.B. (Russian intelligence police). They were visible everywhere. We were in the upper part of the synagogue, the balcony reserved for women. All the women were in their mid-sixties or older. On our way out I stopped to talk with the worshippers. The men conversed with me in Yiddish and cautioned me to be careful. They refused comment on conditions, only saying that they needed *tallisim* and *siddurim*.

When we left, I recognized the K.G.B. men and crossed to speak to them. We conversed in English. I inquired why they attended the services. Was it because they admired the Jewish faith? They had the decency to smile and say they were "keeping order". I soon learned that the K.G.B. men were everywhere. Not only I, but Russians as well, had a strange way of walking. Every few moments we turned around to see who and how many were following.

The tragedy of the Russian people is that they live in perpetual fear. No one trusts anyone else. One evening we were watching television in what served as a living, dining and bedroom in Shoshana's apartment. It was a program directed viciously towards Israel. Although I did not speak Russian, the venom came through, and I protested. Present with us was Shoshana, her husband, their daughter and their grandniece. Shoshana rose excitedly and called me into the kitchen. "Please, you must not voice any complaint. It can reach the K.G.B."

"But no one is here," I said. "Yes, my grandniece is. She might be a spy," answered Shoshana.

Often in taxis, my niece would have the driver stop to let us out before we reached our destination. This was because I was forever engaging others in the cab in conversation. When I asked her why we got out, it was always, "The driver might be a spy." I then learned to limit my taxi conversations to the beauty of the country (which by the way was true) and to how "happy" the people seemed to be. As soon as we reached home, a large pillow was placed over the telephone. We hoped that assured our privacy.

One evening we were dinner guests with Canadian friends. Late at night a storm came up, and we could not get a taxi. I asked if it would be possible for us to spend the night since members of the family were away, and there was room. Our hostess admitted that it was out of the question, for in order for me to spend the night in a place other than my niece's apartment I would require permission from Ovir, the Russian immigration office. This was in Moscow, a few streets away from my niece's apartment.

Russia was quite an experience. It taught me to appreciate the freedom of my life in Canada. But in truth it was not so much Russia I had wanted to see; it was Shoshana. I don't think we stopped talking during my entire trip. As far as communism was concerned, we ironed out our views and adjusted our opinions. What I cared most about was that Shoshana had remained Jewish. She took pride in her heritage. For more, I could not ask.

In time I obtained a Canadian visitor's visa for Shoshana. She came to Montreal and during her stay I took her to the cemetery where both my parents were buried. I asked her to say the words father had once pleaded with her to utter. She repeated after me, "Hear, O Israel, the Lord our God, the Lord is One." I felt a sense of freedom. I had discharged my obligation to my father. Shoshana and I wept with regret that my parents had not survived to share this moment.

———————— 🕎 ————————————————————

I must have nurtured in my mind a wish to go to Israel. I don't recall talking about it. One day I said, "I am going to Israel," and I went. I am tied to Israel through my parents. Israel became a part of me as a young girl when I sat at my father's knee. When father uttered the name Israel, he clung to its sound and lingered over it as one does to a rare and precious wine. My father had never relinquished the hope of settling in Israel and at last he made up his mind to do so. He bought land in Israel in the city of Jerusalem, drew a plan for a house and put those plans into action. Sadly, our permits to enter Israel arrived some weeks after father had passed away.

I have been to many countries, some more interesting than others. The most lasting impression was made by Israel. When I boarded the El Al plane, and the stewardess addressed me in Hebrew, I all but swooned for joy. And when we landed, and we all sang "Sholem Aleichem" (peace be with you), I was so excited I tore a valuable necklace of amber beads. I thought such emotions would grip me only on my first trip. Nothing like that. Each time I went, Israel had an even greater effect on me.

On my first arrival my cab driver proved to be interesting and talkative. He was a middle-aged lawyer who had left Germany, but not in time to avoid a concentration camp. He answered my questions of government policy towards the old, questions that had always interested me. And when we came to religious attitudes, he told me a story which he illustrated by driving me to the seat of contention. It proved to be a site where a synagogue was to be constructed. "You see this little building? That synagogue will never be finished. So why? you will ask. I will, being a Jew, simply reply with another question: Why should it be completed? The small congregation for whom it was to be built cannot agree on how to conduct the services. Half are Ashkenazi and the other Sephardim. Both pray in slightly different liturgy. And this is Israel, where no one interferes in religious disputes."

I took every part of Israel to my heart. I made every moment come alive. The Pentateuch has been my companion for years. I followed Abraham, Isaac and Jacob and, most of all, Moses through the Promised Land. The idea of seeing those places had always captured my imagination and held me spellbound. In Israel those Biblical figures accompanied me as I traversed the land.

I took all the tours, then wended my way back by myself to cover the same territory. At one time I joined others in a car. We went to Safad which intrigued me most. It was the seat of *Cabala*, the mysticism that my father had ingrained in me. On our way we saw Israeli soldiers. They were everywhere with their rifles slung over their shoulders. One soldier was seated reading, another was praying. He had on his phylacteries and *tallis*. The *siddur* he held aloft, while he recited the prayers in a low tone, stopping at intervals to gaze up to heaven. Safad was fascinating. We got out of the car, stood on a mountain and gazed up and down. It was so quiet. The streets are narrow with countless steps to climb and little houses of worship nestle everywhere.

I cannot do justice to the beauty of the scenery in Israel. It is breath-taking. One can only say "God, how glorious is this land!" The Israelis took a land infested with marshes and malaria, and they made it into what Moses sold the Jews, "a land of milk and honey". Many times I saw a father and small son, stripped to the waist, working to remove stones from the earth. They worked in rhythm, with a love that was dug into the soil. And that is what made Israel grow.

One tour I was keen to take was Masada. Masada was the last stronghold against the Romans in 73 A.D. It was the end of Jewish independence. There were 960 souls holding out on the high mountain. The siege lasted three years. When the Romans reached Masada, the 960 were dead. They had killed themselves rather than give up their freedom.

We ascended by cable car to the great heights of the ruins which we explored. We were positively overwhelmed with wonder. The remains enabled us to view what had been Herod's palace. How well planned and modern the palace was. Rooms in apartments, a bathhouse and stools to rest after the baths. Water reservoirs, special compartments for food supplies, the place was impregnable.

The tour was finally over. We all got into the cable car. Disaster, the car would not start! We waited, hoping we would be rescued. No such luck. Finally our guide declared we had no alternative but to descend the mountain by foot. We were petrified!

Masada stands two and a half miles from the shore and forty metres above the level of the Mediterranean Sea. There were two paths, the bank and the serpent path. We learned later that our guide was new at his job and was aware of only one path, the serpent one. Narrow, winding, slippery, full of sharp rocks with nothing to hold on to. Certain death if one slipped, and the same if one looked down.

If our guide was inexperienced, he was brave and willing. We would never have made it otherwise. Twice he caught people by their clothing. He would lead one of us a few steps and proceed to the next one. We reached the bottom of the mountain by early nightfall, exhausted but happy to be alive. I spent two days in bed; I could not regain my balance. Masada, never again!

There is so much to see in Jerusalem, that beautiful, historical city. I longed to see the Wailing Wall, the last remnant of the Second Temple and the holiest shrine of Judaism, which at that time was still in possession of Jordan. One Friday before the Sabbath, I walked the streets of Jerusalem, stopping pedestrians to ask if there was a place from which I could catch a glimpse of the Wall. Shades of Moses, I thought. He could not see Canaan, and I could not see the Wall. I was informed there was a high roof which I could reach if I could climb many stairs; I would be permitted to look over and see the Wall. So up the stairs I went, shaded my eyes and saw the Wall.

A place that is close to my heart is the district of Mea Shearim, home of Chassidic Jews in Jerusalem. The best time to visit Mea Shearim is Friday prior to the Sabbath when men, women and children are scrubbed and decked out for the Sabbath. The men are attired in the garments worn in the ghettos of Europe just as my father had been dressed. Oh, I loved seeing those people. My soul and my spirit left my body and danced a *hora* in these streets of Jerusalem. To me, these people are the epitome of Judaism as I knew it in my home.

I am still a woman of missions. In Jerusalem I made my way to a Chassidic yeshiva. At the entrance, I was met by a young student who forthwith covered his eyes when he saw me. This was to avoid temptation. I was amused. I know Abraham's wife conceived Isaac when she was past "the ways of women". However, we were both saved as I had no desire to capture the innocent youngster. One of the rabbis appeared, and I explained my errand. He looked at me with awe as I handed him some of my father's works. He saw father's name and gratefully accepted the gift.

Each trip to Israel is a rebirth, a rededication for me. I love Israel. I walk through the streets and touch the houses. I have grown as the country has. I remember the first trip when I saw a car driven on the Sabbath, and I felt indignation. Now I feel tolerance and love. I have learned that worship is composed of many things. It does not have to consume; it can just give shelter.

# CHAPTER 12

## Reflections

ALWAYS WHEN I AM GREETED with the exclamation, "I read about your famous son," my retort is invariably, "Which one?" I have been endowed with two sons, both prominent and distinguished in their respective careers.

I never interfered in their career choices. I had long ago abandoned the hope of the rabbinate. My older son, Ari, was always interested in optometry and eye diseases in which he later received his doctorate. When Moshe declared he would follow a literary occupation, I was not surprised. We are after all a literary family. After London, England, Moshe left for Paris and later settled on an island in Spain where he wrote his first book. Finally he came home, and we received the exciting news that he had a publisher. We were ecstatic!

There is a joy, an intenseness, a turbulence that accompanies the publication of a first book. I would stand outside the bookshops, entranced by the sight of my son's book. The next step was the daily visit to the shops to inquire casually how sales were going and to stand quietly in a corner and watch purchasers.

Both my sons are strong minded. It was pointless to try to persuade them to change their minds once they had decided on a certain course. We had arguments about religion. They would decide on a festival and fail to observe it. Not out of malice; they cherished a love for the festivals. In reality, it was a deliberate act meant as a show of revolt, an act of freedom achieved through protest. I could understand that well; I identified with it. To me, it indicated their strength of character.

The friends whom the boys cultivated were both Jewish and Gentile. At times my sons would startle me after a fiery discussion on Judaism and threaten me, "Behave or we marry out of the faith." This was always directed towards me with a glance to see how I took it. The truth is I never took it seriously.

I had much to be thankful for. My sons were doing well, and I was at last safe and free from care. Then enter intermarriage! It was like a tornado that burst upon me. I was totally unprepared. Not in the most remote recess of my mind did such a thought occur. For a while there was the anguish of "Where had I failed?" I could not understand how this could happen to sons that were cradled and reared in the lap of Jewish orthodoxy.

Protest, shout, threaten? No, I decided if I did that, I would lose my children. My sons were, after all, grown men and free to make their own choices. So I tried to accept and understand. It was painful, but eventually it dawned on me that I had only considered myself. It had not occurred to me that I was anti-Gentile as some Gentiles were anti-Jewish. Nor had I considered that the parents of my sons' wives felt the same pain I did, that their children were marrying out of their faith. I had been bigoted and intolerant. When I understood this, I began to regard my sons' wives as equals, to accept them with the hope that they would bestow the same consideration on me. There were moments of despair, probably for all of us, but ultimately we developed a relationship based on mutual regard and deep affection.

I am old now. However I do not feel any different from when I was young. Old age is reputed to be trying. No such thing. I feel no less agile, not the least decrepit, and positively no inward transformations have occurred. I am as well as I ever was. I run to catch a bus. I exercise, walk as quick as the wind. There is a lilt to my body. I have had many illnesses, considerable surgery, but age did not prevent immediate recovery. It was just one more hill to climb. My mind is alert, sharp as a razor edge, more so with each passing year. I find old age a time of awareness, response and appreciation. I am beginning to wonder what this fuss concerning old age is all about.

Am I fooling myself? No, the debit side is ever before me. Outwardly, the body changes. One has to force oneself to look into the mirror and accept the changes. The wrinkles and sagging muscles denote diverse paths in our lives. But there is even an awesome beauty there. I gaze into the eyes of other old people, and reflected is a wealth of wisdom. To fight those changes is merely to face defeat. People want to live long but not to grow old. It does not work that way. We live in a youth-oriented society. How ridiculous this is. The pathetic effort to look young only serves to accentuate age and robs us of the beauty and grace that age can bring us.

When age descends, one must decide on certain observances. For example, one has to accept the necessity of keeping oneself scrupulously clean, to take pride in one's appearance. It is of the utmost importance in the older years. I find pleasure in exploring cosmetic counters for delightfully scented soaps, deodorants and mouthwashes. I do not tolerate boredom or self pity in myself. I will not conform to the monotony of doing the same things day after day, nor eating the same food, nor thinking the same thoughts nor even shopping in the same places. I want to enhance my life with pleasant excitements.

I am constantly on guard for flaws that may occur due to age so that I can overcome or at least understand whatever I can. I was upset when I had difficulty in recalling certain words or names of objects. I soon learned that the mind comes to the rescue in a few moments. I was determined to find out why. My older son furnished me with literature titled "Long and Short-Term Memory".

Have I no fears? There are so many that I have stopped counting them. I am no paragon of strength and fortitude. Most frightening of all is loneliness. While we strive to make peace with old age, the factor that plays the most devastating part in our lives is loneliness. It is gnawing, the most acute deprivation. For it is not money, nor health that is so vital. It is loved ones. Those can never be replaced.

An old friend confided that she goes to a supermarket, drinks coffee and sits for hours just to come in contact with others. Another older woman told me, "When my phone rings, I often don't answer. I know it's a wrong number. It never rings for me." They both uttered the same cry, "What shall I do today?" I was overcome with sadness. More than ever I realize the necessity of acquiring reserves for our older years. No, I am not immune to depression and pain. I fight loneliness till it passes. I lean on my memories; that is my life line. It represents a savings account that I can draw on.

Am I afraid to die? I can honestly say no. What I fear is *how* I will die. I hope not to linger but to die with dignity as I have tried to live. Death is as much a part of life as living. When a life is conceived, it comes forth inevitably. When life is over, it ends inevitably. I am prone to think that death may even be a great adventure. However, I hope to curtail my curiosity for a while.

I decided to purchase a cemetery plot as close to my parents as I could financially manage. My brother went with me to make arrangements at the chapel. In charge was an older rabbi. First I told him, "The chapel is very dark. Please, when my body is brought in, put all the lights on. I detest darkness." Poor man, he eyed me suspiciously. Reluctantly he produced the map and tried to sell me a plot at the edge of the cemetery. I said, "No deal, Rabbi. I don't want to be stepped on by those who visit graves. I did not like being stepped on in my lifetime. Shall I now give up in my death?" His face was a study. I detected a sense of fear. He thought he was in the presence of a dangerous female. I emerged laughing. I thought, here I am buying a burial plot. Surely I should feel sombre. But no, I was convulsed with mirth. I wondered if that was the first sign of senility.

All through life I have been an early riser; now I am even more so. In the summer six in the morning is glorious. The air is fresh. I am out in the garden weeding and examining rosebushes, vegetables and tomato plants. The time is mine. I can now do as I please. It is no longer necessary to compete for a place in this world or suffer poverty or endure an unhappy marriage or worry about the children. I am so thankful that my years of deprivation took place while I was still of an age to combat them.

And there is the gratification of grandchildren. The greatest arias are not as musical as the sounds of *"bube"* (grandmother). I respond to their calls with an emotion that engulfs me. My heart stands still as I look at them. When my oldest grandson came with my granddaughter to announce her pregnancy, I danced and shouted and hugged the expectant mother till the child begged for mercy.

Regardless of my age, I shall continue to accept challenges — to climb high mountains with my face against the wind. But I have achieved a measure of peace. I have made strides to suit my needs. Basically my values remain the same, only modified. They had to enable me to meet the challenge of the present. I had to embrace the times we live in, so that I could move unhampered in both worlds, the old and the new. The richness, the foliage of my heritage and my roots are the legacy of my parents. I have carried my heritage with love and dignity and always will. Therein lies my strength. My roots have endowed me with a wealth of feelings that have always stood by me. And I am deeply grateful. I cling to my faith and my beliefs not because they make life easier, rather that they make life better, richer, more worthwhile. I live and breathe with hope that my heritage will not perish with me, for there is no greater gift can I pass on to my children and theirs!

# Glossary

The orthography of Yiddish and Hebrew words that have been transliterated into English varies widely. The following books were used as reference guides:

Kogos, Fred. *A Dictionary of Yiddish Slang & Idoms*. Secaucus: Castle Books, 1978.

Rosenbaum, Samuel. *A Yiddish Work Book for English-Speaking People*. New York: Van Nostrand Reinhold Company, 1978.

Rosten, Leo. *The Joys of Yiddish*. New York: Pocket Books, 1968.

Roth, Cecil. *The Concise Jewish Encyclopedia*. New York: New American Library, 1980.

*afikomen*   piece of matzo used for dessert at the
   Passover Seder
*alter heym*   old home
*am ha-aretz*   people of the land
*arbes*   chickpeas
*baal tfileh*   conductor of prayer services
*badchen*   jester, master of ceremonies at a
   wedding
*bakoshe*   request
*bris*   circumcision
*bube*   grandmother
*bucher*   bachelor
*Cabala*   Jewish mystical teaching
*challah*   braided bread
*charoses*   mixture of apples, nuts and wine
*Chassidism*   Jewish religious mystical movement
   founded in Eastern Europe in the eighteenth
   century
*cheder*   school or classroom where Hebrew is
   taught
*chometz*   leaven, any food containing leaven
   forbidden on Passover
*chuppa*   wedding canopy, marriage ceremony
   itself
*Din Torah*   Jewish court of settlement based on
   the Laws of the Torah
*drusha geshunk*   wedding presents
*dybbuk*   evil spirit
*eileh*   genius
*esrog*   citron
*gartel*   black belt made of silk twine worn by
   religious Jews
*gefilte fish*   fish patties
*gesheft*   business
*get*   bill of divorce
*goy (s), goyim (pl)*   non-Jew(s)
*greener*   newcomer, immigrant
*gut shabbes*   greeting for the Sabbath
*habdala*   benedictions said at the conclusion of
   the Sabbath

*Haggadah*   narrative read aloud at the Passover
  Seder
*hora*   Jewish folk dance
*iberbet*   feather blanket
*kalef*   dog
*kalleh*   bride
*kapote*   long coat worn by Chassidic Jews
*kashrut*   Kosher Laws
*kest*   dowry (room and board)
*Ketubah*   marriage contract
*kichel*   small cookies
*Kiddush*   blessing over wine that sanctifies the
  Sabbath and Jewish holy days, ceremony that
  includes the saying of the *Kiddush* and
  refreshments
*kittel*   white cotton coat worn by religious Jews
*Kohen*   descendant of a member of ancient
  priestly caste
*kop*   head
*kosher (verb)*   to cleanse according to Kosher
  Laws
*landsleit*   societies of people from the same town
*lechter*   Sabbath candlesticks
*lulav*   palm branch
*matzo tash*   cover for unleavened bread
*Megillah*   Book of Esther
*melamed*   teacher
*mezuzah*   prayer (Hear O Israel) that is fastened
  to doorposts of Jewish homes
*mikva*   ritual bath
*Mishnah*   part of the Talmud
*Mishput Hashalom*   court of arbitration, part of
  permanent system of Din Torah
*mitnagid (s), mitnagdim (pl)*   opponent(s) of
  Chassidism
*mitzva*   good deed
*mohel*   circumciser
*nadan*   dowry (money)
*nagid*   wealthy man
*nebech*   someone to be pitied

*ness*  miracle
*oyrech (s), oyrechim (pl)*  guest(s)
*payess*  side earlocks
*pitem*  protruding top of citron
*Polishe*  Polish Jews
*rebbe*  religious leader of a Chassidic community
  not necessarily ordained, often taking up an
  inherited position
*rebbitsin*  wife of rebbe
*Seder*  festive meal of the first two nights of
  Passover
*Shabbes*  Sabbath
*shadchen (m), shadchante (f)*  matchmaker
*shalosh seudot*  the third Sabbath meal eaten late
  Saturday afternoon
*shammes*  errand runner, caretaker of the
  synagogue
*shaytl*  wig
*schechita*  ritual slaughter
*Sedrah*  portion of weekly reading from the
  Pentateuch
*sheriim*  leftovers
*shidech (s), shiduchim (pl)*  match(es)
*shif bruder*  ship brother
*shif shvester*  ship sister
*shifs karten*  passage fare, ship tickets
*shiksa*  Gentile woman
*shister*  shoemaker
*shlachmunus*  gifts
*shnaps*  whisky or any intoxicating drink
*shofar*  ram's horn used on the Jewish new year
*sholem aleichem*  peace be with you
*shoychet (s), shoychtim (pl)*  ritual slaughterer(s)
*shtetl*  village
*shtibl*  makeshift synagogue over store
*shtreimel*  round hat, trimmed with fur worn by
  Chassidic Jews
*siddur (s), siddurim (pl)*  prayer book(s)
*smicha*  rabbinical diploma
*sopher*  Hebrew scribe
*sphorim*  books

*succah*   decorated booth used during the festival
   of Succot
*tallis*   prayer shawl
*tallis kuten*   small prayer shawl
*Talmud*   authoritative compilation and
   discussion of Jewish civil and religious law
*trayf*   non-kosher
*Tseno-Ureno*   book or volumes of Yiddish
   writings paraphrased from the Pentateuch,
   usually read by women on the Sabbath
*tsholent*   casserole of potatoes, meat and beans
*tzaddik*   righteous man, miracle worker
*tzedaka*   charity
*tzigezoogt*   promises
*tzitzis*   fringes at the corners of the prayer shawl
*und yener*   and the other one
*yeshiva*   Jewish school for higher learning,
   Talmudic academy
*yeshiva bucher*   male student of Talmudic
   academy
*yiches*   family status or prestige
*yiddishe shiksa*   Jewish-Gentile lady, character
   on a radio program
*yiddishkeit*   Jewishness, Jewish tradition
*yidele*   little Jew with a long beard
*yingelech*   little boys
*zaftig*   juicy, plump, buxom
*zaide*   grandfather
*Zohar*   most influential Cabalist text